T0300275

ROUTLEDGE LIBRARY EDITIONS:
INDUSTRIAL RELATIONS

Volume 19

INDUSTRIAL RELATIONS IN A CHANGING WORLD

INDUSTRIAL RELATIONS IN A CHANGING WORLD

Edited by
MICHAEL E. BEESLEY

Routledge
Taylor & Francis Group

LONDON AND NEW YORK

First published in 1975 by Croom Helm Ltd.

This edition first published in 2025
by Routledge
4 Park Square, Milton Park, Abingdon, Oxon OX14 4RN

and by Routledge
605 Third Avenue, New York, NY 10158

Routledge is an imprint of the Taylor & Francis Group, an informa business

© 1975 Michael Beesley

All rights reserved. No part of this book may be reprinted or reproduced or utilised in any form or by any electronic, mechanical, or other means, now known or hereafter invented, including photocopying and recording, or in any information storage or retrieval system, without permission in writing from the publishers.

Trademark notice: Product or corporate names may be trademarks or registered trademarks, and are used only for identification and explanation without intent to infringe.

British Library Cataloguing in Publication Data
A catalogue record for this book is available from the British Library

ISBN: 978-1-032-81770-5 (Set)
ISBN: 978-1-032-81713-2 (Volume 19) (hbk)
ISBN: 978-1-032-81730-9 (Volume 19) (pbk)
ISBN: 978-1-003-50107-7 (Volume 19) (ebk)

DOI: 10.4324/9781003501077

Publisher's Note
The publisher has gone to great lengths to ensure the quality of this reprint but points out that some imperfections in the original copies may be apparent.

Disclaimer
The publisher has made every effort to trace copyright holders and would welcome correspondence from those they have been unable to trace.

THE STOCKTON LECTURES, 1974

INDUSTRIAL RELATIONS IN A CHANGING WORLD

EDITED BY

MICHAEL BEESLEY

CROOM HELM LONDON

CRANE, RUSSAK NEW YORK

© 1975 by Michael Beesley

Croom Helm Ltd.
2−10 St. Johns Road, London SW 11

ISBN 0−85664−296−7

Published in the United States by
Crane, Russak & Company Inc.
347 Madison Avenue,
New York, N.Y. 10017

Printed by Biddles of Guildford

CONTENTS

EDITOR'S FOREWORD

In these turbulent times for industrial relations and government policy many of the events referred to in the chapters that follow already seem a long way off. The first three were written just as the confrontation between the government's prices and wages policy and trade union's commitment to a voluntary bargaining system was coming to a peak. While they were delivered as lectures at the school, between January and March 1974, the general election, called on the issue of relations between unions and government, and the government's defeat, came and went. While the book was being prepared for publication, the social contract, embodying the idea of voluntary wage restraint in return for political action, became the linch-pin of government policy, and was given a further lease by the second general election in 1974. At the time this is written, the social contract's meaning, its progress and its possible future are hotly disputed, while the economic background in which bargaining takes place has worsened at a speed without precedent.

Yet the more quickly events crowd in, the more important it is to have a strong framework within which to interpret them. Industrial relations embrace very deep-rooted attitudes and institutions. Change, if it is to be radical, is slow. The papers expose long-term trends underlying current developments and, we hope, contribute significantly to the building of the framework for argument. They emphasise, for example, the importance and variety of objective industrial conditions that condition bargaining, the capacity of bargaining machinery to absorb change, the long-standing ideology inherent in the social contract, the gradual emergence of a multinational dimension in trade union affairs, and the structural difficulties facing companies (and unions) who wish to elevate participation in company affairs to a leading role in industrial relations.

Thus, our idea in selecting the 1974 Stockton lectures was to ask four active representatives of very different roles in industrial relations to reflect on the future as they saw it — the independent conciliator,

7

a major British trade union, a large company known for its care about employer-employee relations, and a leading international trade union organisation. Except for the last, this indeed has been accomplished. The first three chapters are statements of those deeply involved, not to say embattled, in the industrial relations scene. Even apart from their analytical, reflective content, they are useful evidence about what concerned people in significant positions at the time. Sir Leonard Neal wrote from his experience as Chairman of the Commission on Industrial Relations, a leading force in bargaining, but so soon to be a casualty of changing policy; Mr. Alan Fisher represented the viewpoint of a general section of an extremely influential union, and Mr. Adrian Cadbury spoke as the Deputy Chairman of a company with a long tradition of innovation in personnel relations. Because the planned fourth lecture could not, in the event, be delivered, Mr. Larry Whitty was asked to contribute an essay covering the same ground. He brings together the many and complex strands comprising unions' response to the growth of multinational companies. As the research officer of a major union he has been deeply concerned with this for some years. His exposition shows how international cooperation in the trade union — as in any other sphere — reflects, and depends upon, the capabilities for organisation within the constituent countries. Thus the concerns and the several viewpoints of the first three authors reappear, sometimes in different forms, in the developments he describes. It also seemed appropriate to ask Mr. Andrew Gottschalk, lecturer in industrial relations at the London Business School, to comment on the four contributions. He does this in Chapter 5, setting the contributions against the changing emphases during the last ten years upon voluntary collective bargaining, government intervention in wages and prices and the enlarging area of practical bargaining and participation issues.

The United Kingdom, for better or worse, has a more open economy than at any other time in its history. Irrespective of formal attachment, or possible detachment, from particular trading partners or political groups, it is steadily increasing its interdependence with other economies. Its economic institutions respond and develop accordingly. Compared with our international partners, formalised bargaining, and trade unions in particular, cover an exceptional proportion of the work-force. The quality of the UK's economic performance will owe not a little to how far our own industrial relations structure and the institutions comprising it can anticipate needs, rather than lag behind manifest ones. But these institutions, perhaps especially in the UK, are social institutions too. How social and economic ambitions are reconciled is the key issue for the next decade. The UK's industrial relations institutions will have a unique opportunity, as well as responsibility, to influence social and economic choice. We hope that the essays that follow will make a useful contribution to founding those choices in rational argument, for the Stockton Lectures were themselves conceived to explore the balance of social and economic concerns at which western economies should aim.

All connected with the lectures were greatly saddened by the sudden death of their founder, Mr. Eli Goldston, in January 1974. He remarked, in his preface to the first volume of Stockton Lectures upon his father's capacity 'to do well by doing good'. He himself had this quality to an extraordinary degree. One reflects that his quite exceptional empathy, his genius for finding novel solutions to problems, and, not least, his clear-sighted optimism, would not only have produced trenchant observations on these papers, but also some imaginative and practical lines of development for our consideration. But we can at least be glad that the debate has been pushed forward in some measure by his generosity in providing for the occasion of this book.

We are also grateful to the contributors, who, apart from putting so much into preparing themselves, provided the occasions for most interesting discussions after the lectures.

Michael Beesley

1. NEW THINKING AND ACTION IN INDUSTRIAL RELATIONS

Sir Leonard Neal

In this lecture I am to answer the question, 'What new thinking and action in industrial relations is required from industry, unions, government and other groups (e.g. consumers, media, etc.)?'. The question 'what?' of course, is less difficult than 'how?'. In addressing myself to these questions I shall give my personal views alone. Nothing that I say should be assumed to represent the opinions of the Commission on Industrial Relations. The *problem* of industrial relations is one that can be stated with great ease — but it is (perhaps) a problem that no one should be asked to solve — men, wise and learned in these matters, have discerned in 'industrial relations' a system, a rhythm — almost a predetermined pattern. But these harmonies are concealed from ordinary people who are conscious only of one industrial crisis following another. And indeed that is the reality of the continuing situation — of increasing conflict, hostility and dislocation; of disputes annually disrupting basic industries; of restrictions on output and the retarding of innovation. It is an enigma that has exercised our minds for seventy years or more.

It is interesting to recall some comments of Sidney Webb about seventy years ago on these same matters —

'I cannot accept the assumption that a system of organised struggles between employers and workmen, leading inevitably now and again to strikes and lockouts represents the only method or even a desirable method by which to settle the conditions of employment. A strike or a lockout necessarily involves so much individual suffering, so much injury to third parties and so much national loss, that it cannot, in my opinion, be accepted as the normal way of settling an intractable dispute. Moreover, from the standpoint of the community, such a method has the drawback that it affords no security that the resultant conditions of employment will not be gravely injurious to the community as a whole; I cannot believe that a civilised community will permanently continue to abandon the adjustment of industrial disputes — and incidentally the regulation of the conditions of life of the mass of the people — to what is, in reality, the arbitrament of war'*

The quality of industrial relations in our society is now worsening, and at such a rate, that some sober commentators believe that it contains within it the possibility of undermining our social system itself. I am bound to say that I do not take that melancholy view of the situation. But this decline will not respond merely to optimism, no matter how large the doses; nor, of course, will it do other than deepen if the dynamic of conflict is answered only by the inertia of indifference. There are still too many who positively encourage strife in trade ingenuous belief that better social orders flow from the use of conflict; and on the other hand there are those who take refuge in a sort of far-Eastern fatalism that 'it will all come right after a collapse' — both economic and social. Again, I reject such simplistic concepts. There is, and there will remain for many years, an urgent need to give our minds to the problem of reform and improvement, to remove the defects and the excesses — for I see no comfort or future by way of an industrial armageddon.

The Changing Nature of Industrial Conflict

As Sidney Webb noted, conflict and disputation are endemic in the industrial situation, but, as he also argued, we should beware of so emphasising the virtues and inevitability of conflict that we are overwhelmed by it. The support that has been given to conflict in industry in the last twenty years has produced two major disquieting features — firstly, as to the scale of conflict and, secondly, as to its intensity and aggressiveness.

i. Scale

As to the first of these features — 'scale' — the figures speak for

*Précis of Sidney Webb's Addendum to the Royal Commission on Trade Disputes of 1903-6.

themselves:

	1950	1960	1969	1970	1971	1972
No. of strikes p.a.	600	1,600	2,900	3,750	2,093	2,252
Man-days lost p.a.	1.4m.	3m.	8m.	11m.	13.6m.	24m.

There can be no doubt that we have become a more disputatious nation in these last years, especially as these figures do not even reveal the dislocation caused by more limited industrial action such as the work-to-rule, prohibition of overtime, sit-ins etc. For example, in the motor industry it has been estimated that nearly one million cars were lost to production in 1973 by these latter causes alone.

ii Intensity

Strikes, of course, have never been pleasant affairs but they have been modified in the past by the sort of early nineteenth-century behaviour that characterised the outbreak of hostilities between nations. It was generally acknowledged then that there were certain rules of the game that precluded the taking of unfair advantage of the community. Thus, many industrial disputants would take account of the impact their quarrel had on the welfare of others. Essential services *would* be maintained. Hospital needs *would* be met. The sick, the aged and schoolchildren *would not* be hostages in a battle to which they were not a party.

But in many dispute situations these standards no longer obtain. The strike has, somehow, acquired a morality of its own which appears to make any interruption of work justifiable, irrespective of its purposes and heedless of its methods. The 'right' in some instances to strike has been elevated to such a status, and has been talked about and stressed to such an extent by the few, that the two words have become confused and a strike becomes 'right' merely because it is a strike. Thus, attempts by others to exercise *their* rights in relation to any particular strike are stigmatised as 'strike-breaking' and, according to the new morality, such behaviour is unpardonable and must be frustrated at all costs. Thus tomato-growers must not be allowed to air-lift their products into the country

12

from the Channel Islands during a dock strike; clerical workers and safety engineers are reviled as blacklegs in the 1972 mining strike and volunteer ambulance drivers taking emergency cases to hospital are obstructed and derided in 1973.

Thus not only has the scale of disputation increased but it has been coupled with a new kind of nastiness as well.

The Origins of Increased Conflict

The reasons for this disturbed and disturbing situation are complex and manifold and it is not likely that there will be unanimity as to the diagnosis. Nevertheless, some factors seem to be significant. Some are fundamental as sources of conflict, while others are incidental in that they may not (in themselves) be the causes of conflict but they tend to exacerbate already tense situations. *All* seem to have come together at about the same point in time.

In a contradictory way the removal of earlier social defects seems likely itself to be a prime cause of conflict. In pre-war years it was believed that if only we could remove some of the worst social blemishes such as poverty, insecurity, secular unemployment, inequity in the distribution of power, income, and educational opportunities then conflict would melt away like the snow in summer. To a large extent these blemishes have been removed. Secular unemployment has given way to much higher levels of employment; much poverty has been replaced by relative affluence; our greatly expanded university system is crowded with the children of working-class families; power is no longer the exclusive possession of bankers, ministers or managers, but is much more widely dispersed throughout society.

The consequence of all these social, economic and political changes has been to increase the expectations of people and, indeed, to raise those expectations to a much higher level than society can meet. The ensuing failure to understand the inherent limitations and the frustration of those same ambitious expectations has thus been a potent source of much recent conflict.

13

The post-war period has seen a fantastic development in the methods of production. The demand for consumer goods has led to a great increase in mass production methods so that entire processes have become acutely interdependent. An operation becomes not only dependent on the one before but it is sensitive also to the one that follows. A breakdown of any operation ensures chaos at many other places elsewhere along the line. A strike or stoppage affecting a relatively small supplier or a small department has a greatly disproportionate effect on the whole enterprise, and manufacturing industry has in consequence become vulnerable to industrial conflict.

One of the strangest phenomena of the world of post-war affluence is that we now live in an age when every form of violence has its intellectual apologists. The virtues of conflict, if not of violence, are extolled even in some social science departments. Conflict, we are told, is necessary to remedy an intolerable situation, to destroy apathy and inertia. Out of the clash of interests and wills new ideas and new orders develop. The new demagogues understand that 'he, who seeketh to persuade the multitude that they are not well governed, shall not lack an audience.' The ferment of unrest generated by excessive ambitions has thus been skillfully exploited by those wishing to see extreme social change.

The working man, however, is not a wild-eyed malevolent revolutionary. By and large 99 per cent of the work-force is reasonable, wanting merely to get a good day's pay for its work. It wants, in addition, an improving standard of life, increasing satisfaction at the workplace and, above most things, to be intelligently, fairly and firmly led. It dislikes vacillation, indecision and lack of authority and it reserves its profoundest contempt for those who display weakness when they should have been firm and unyielding. It will accept leadership — particularly from conventional quarters, if that leadership is firm as well as fair. But if this work-force makes claims that it knows to be excessive and are met with weakness from authority, then it will exploit that weakness with unholy glee. And this is what we have seen so frequently in recent years — the continued success of militancy based on the continuing weakness of those

14

who should have displayed firmness — in management, in government and in the unions. For workpeople this retreat has had only one lesson — that militancy pays. That it might *appear* to pay only in the short term and that in the long term it would be self-defeating are arguments that workers find, in practice, wholly unconvincing.

Many people have a childlike faith in the advantages of so-called free, voluntary collective bargaining. (And, of course, this 'collective bargaining' is thought to be better still if can be pursued at the level of the industry.) The Donovan Commission, The Industrial Relations Act, 1971; the Code of Industrial Relations Practice all regard it as self-evident that 'good industrial relations' flow from the principle of collective bargaining freely conducted on behalf of workers and employers. To be fair, the Act does go on to say that such a principle cannot be separated from the general interests of the community. It is, however, difficult to find much evidence that this latter qualification engages the attention of the negotiators to any great extent. If the qualification is remembered, by either side, it is only to emphasise that the interests of the community are identical with one or other of the parties that happens to have remembered it. Dr. John Dunlop of the Harvard Business School goes further and asserts that 'collective bargaining contributes much to what has been called the permanent efficiency of the nation.'

But these touching affirmations of faith in the advantages of collective bargaining (certainly as presently practised in the UK) are difficult to reconcile with the facts. It is doubtful whether free collective bargaining has diminished conflict in industry; or whether it has, of itself, produced any general gains in real wages over that which has been secured by rising productivity. It has contributed nothing to the problem of the low-paid — as Michael Stewart of London University has testified; and in recent years it has almost certainly been one significant factor in the level of unemployment, as the table overleaf may suggest.

It is difficult to avoid the conclusion that the system of free bargaining has, firstly, not been coping with the effects of the social political and economic changes of recent years and, secondly, it produces no convincing evidence that a free and completely

15

Year	Average Increase in Weekly Wage Rates	Average Level of Unemployment
1950-66	2.0% p.a.	1.6% p.a.
1967	2.1% p.a.	2.2% p.a.
1968	7.4% p.a.	2.4% p.a.
1969	5.0% p.a.	2.6% p.a.
1970	8.0% p.a.	2.6% p.a.
1971	13.0% p.a.	3.6% p.a.
1972	12.1% p.a.	4.0% p.a.

(Source: *Department of Employment Gazette*)

unregulated system will in the long term produce the right blend of
benefits for the entire community. In an interdependent community
the opportunity to exploit sectional powers poses a very real danger
that operates eventually to the detriment of the community as a
whole. The irony of the present situation is that, in terms of total
public welfare some form of 'regulatory conservatism' seems to have
more relevance than *'laisser faire* socialism'. At a time when a
Conservative Government is pursuing policies that interfere with
market forces, an avowedly socialist trade union movement is
extolling the advantages of 'the theory of the market!'

The market may be, in theory, the primary mechanism for the
allocation of resources but time and the convenience of people will
not wait for these market forces to operate.

It is a melancholy experience to read the debates, at some annual
conferences, on the economic problem. We have speakers who claim
the following: all workers are underpaid but all want a more
equitable distribution of income; parity with higher-paid workers
is essential but so also is the maintenance of differentials; many must
be treated as 'special cases' but miners, dockers, car workers, printers,
train drivers and craftsmen in general must all be at the top of the
wages league; there must be greater stability in prices but attempts
to do this via income and prices policies interfere with the processes
of free collective bargaining; for good measure there must be more for
pensioners, more social security, lower taxes, economic growth and

16

full employment. To be fair, of course, there are also voices that question the conventional wisdom. For instance Mr. Chapple enquires:

'We demand control of key prices such as food, housing, rents, fuel, fares; we call for larger family allowances and pension increases, and action to raise the earnings of the lower-paid. Therefore, it surely cannot be reasonable to insist on totally unrestricted voluntary collective bargaining; and what is more, if our complaints about the scandalously low pay of any group of organised workers are correct – and I am certain that they are – does not free collective bargaining share some responsibility for their position? If the case that is being put here for parity is correct, will not its achievement also affect free collective bargaining, if we are all to have the same rates of pay in the differing circumstances in which we all work?'

Mr. Jackson is even more emphatic:

'We can see no merit in the slogan: "Back Free Collective Bargaining", because collective bargaining is not free, and has never been free as far as public service workers are concerned. It is not collective, because we will not do it together. It is not bargaining, unless you have enormous industrial strength to back up your arguments. There is nothing marvellous about free collective bargaining. It has got nothing to do with Socialism. It is a complete acceptance of the capitalist ethos. Free collective bargaining means poverty for many people in this country, and it is time that we stopped pretending that free collective bargaining has cured any of our particular problems.'

And it is not only trade union debates to which I refer. We can be assured that the study of reports from employers' association meetings provide an adequate balance to those of those trade unions. But it is doubtful if this is the sort of equilibrium we are looking for!

New Thought and Action

The third part of this paper directs attention to the nature of new thought and action on the part of government, management, trade

17

unions and others. It may not be possible literally to fulfil this requirement, particularly concerning the adjective 'new'. I cannot be sure that the kind of prescriptions that follow my diagnosis are all utterly new. Some may have a seminal quality and others certainly less so. But all are new so far as their application is concerned over large areas of both sides of industry. Notwithstanding the clamour of critics within and outside the trade union movement, I expect that the law will continue to exercise a profound influence on industrial relations and on collective bargaining. It seems to me quite profoundly mistaken to assume that these two activities are independent of one another, and that non-legal improvements can be sought in one which will in some way rub off on the other.

i. *Income and Prices Policies*

It does not seem to be a repudiation of the capitalist ethic to assert that, from time to time, the most extreme excesses of the market should yield to the restraints of the community law. Britain is too overcrowded, too dependant on imports, too sensitive to the vagaries of world trade for it to be able, over the long term, to rely exclusively on the doctrines of a market economy. If we did we should be utterly vulnerable to the pressures that power groups inside and outside can exert upon us. Without the constraints of a framework of law we would be in real danger of bargaining ourselves out of vital markets and it seems certain, therefore, that present and previous attempts to develop forms of incomes policies will continue — for the determination of wage and salary settlements cannot be left entirely to the outcome of free collective bargaining. Whether or not we have been successful now or in the more distant past is hardly the point, for free bargaining is not an unqualified truth that lies at one end of the economic spectrum (where all veracity exists) while at the other end lies the dark spectre of interventionism surrounded by error, bureaucracy, unfairness and other marks of the devil. In fact, in our overstretched economies the truth will lie somewhere near the middle — sometimes moving a little to the left and at other times, nearer to the right. In the long term we shall, I suppose, adhere to the standards of free enterprise, based on rewards for incentive and effort but with an occasional touch on the brake that will be applied whether governments in Whitehall are Conservative or whether they are Labour.

It is, therefore, in the nature of 'incomes policies' in a free society that they are inevitable but that they are likely also to be short-run affairs. I think that such policies in the United Kingdom will continue to appear, continue to be short-run, continue to be 'different' and continue to be the same! The achievement of greater equilibrium in wage bargaining however, does not have to be seen in terms of permanent forms of incomes policy with all the inherent possibilities of ever-larger bureaucracies concerned in their administration. The continuing problem in a free society is that of achieving the right sort of balance between economic growth, increasing living standards, reduced inflation, long-term stability in our overseas payments — and to do all these conflicting things while reducing interference in industry to the minimum. (It may be said, in this context, that the simultaneous pursuit of diametrically opposite solutions is likely to lead to difficulties — as we have found!)

Nevertheless, this must be our objective — to maximise both freedom and order for neither freedom nor order can in the long run live without the other. And one way that might be considered for achieving the maximum degree of freedom in collective bargaining is to see whether we can construct a national system of conciliation and arbitration by isolating the factors that appear to contribute more than others to the volatility of collective bargaining. It seems that these factors include a widespread confusion about the facts in the arguments of both sides; about mistrust of arbitration; and the quite subjective attempts to enlist the support of the public by one or other of the parties.

Now the curious paradox about 'facts' is that arguments about them are the most bitter, time-consuming and destructive and yet at the same time 'facts', by definition, are the one element in the whole situation that can be put beyond the realm of disputation. One can engage in arguments until the end of time, and with almost theological intensity, about the position that a group of workers should occupy in the wages league, but facts about their average

19

wages and their position, presently and previously in the wages league can be established without any difficulty at all. Similarly, arguments about the costs of particular claims and the impact on the price of products and services can equally be objectively estimated. But these are the very areas where the greatest arguments lie and which thus provide the mainspring from which so much of the ensuing bitterness is released. Somehow the public interest has to be involved in major wage bargains at a much earlier stage than is the case now and the facts have to be established before opinions have hardened and uncompromising attitudes have been struck.

A further little-noticed 'fact' is that wage bargaining patterns tend to be established during each annual wage-round by a relatively small number of strategically important industries. And even within industries a similar tendency exists for one company or a part of a company to be the pace-setters. It is therefore possible that major wage bargains likely to have a large predictable impact on the economy, or likely to be significantly repercussive throughout an entire industry could be identified in advance. There could then be appointed to the bargaining sessions, from the beginning, an independent fact-finder, whose task would be to determine the facts *with the parties.* These facts could then be widely communicated to all concerned. Such a system might work in the following way:

1. A list of 'independent fact-finders' could be drawn up after consultation with the CBI and the TUC. Such a list would include lawyers, economists, consultants, ex-managers and ex-trade union officials.
2. Appropriate criteria would need to be agreed as to when a particular set of negotiations warranted the attention of an 'independent fact-finder'.
3. The role of the 'independent fact-finder' in such situations would be primarily to determine the facts and secure the agreement of the parties as to those facts and to advise the public (including the employees who are represented). In this way 'the 3rd party' would be inserted into potentially difficult situations at the beginning rather than as a *'deus ex machina'*

at the end when the combatants are eyeball to eyeball with one another.

4. The criteria would be primarily concerned with an individual wage bargain that was thought to have significant repercussive possibilities in other important industries e.g. engineering, motor-car employment, municipal employment etc. But the criteria could also be concerned with a sectional claim that was considered likely to reverberate throughout a large company or industry. It would also be important, from the public point of view, to include amongst the criteria the duty to consider the likely effect on prices of the product or services involved by any proposed claim or possible settlement.

5. None of this, of course, would preclude the government of the day from indicating what its concept of the year's norm or maximum for increases in incomes should be.

The suggestion of an 'independent fact-finder', to be present at significant wage claims, could be extremely valuable in preventing attitudes from hardening. Moreover, it would be extremely difficult to repudiate his views on the boundaries of the argument in the light of his duty to lay before the public (including the employees concerned) the facts in each case. The expenses need not be great for it is only a few cases each year that contain a high element of pace-setting possibilities.

None of the above should be seen as an argument in favour of automatic, compulsory arbitration on wage matters. Such a practice causes even a positive relationship between the parties to atrophy since if recourse is too frequently made to automatic arbitration, nothing is lost by squeezing the most that can be obtained at the penultimate stage and then proceeding to arbitration in the hope that some further advantage may be extracted. And, since it would effectively remove the right to strike, a compulsory procedure would not secure trade union support either and would also be potentially explosive. There is, however, a great deal to be said for the proposition that when recourse is *jointly* made to voluntary arbitration the award should be regarded by the parties as binding.

These arguments may not be foolproof — nothing this side of the grave ever will be — but they may provide a contribution to a discussion that should now proceed with great urgency if we are to modify our system of collective bargaining within the constraints of a free society.

ii. Participation

This much-used word is in danger of being seen as the new detergent for industrial relations. There is obviously a great deal of advantage that can be obtained from an increase in participation but the concept that it is a universal nostrum runs the risk of being pushed too far. Recently a leading member of Parliament asserted that the establishment of statutory works councils would release a 'tidal wave of enthusiasm for work at the shop-floor level'. One would have thought that members of Parliament, above all others, would be aware of the limitations of the representative system. It is, of course, a valuable method for achieving a greater symmetry in the power structure, but it rarely produces unrestrained joy in the bosoms of the represented. The frequency with which members of Parliament, councillors and shop stewards and other elected or self-appointed representatives are repudiated by those whom they represent, is a vivid testimony to the inevitable chasm that yawns between the electors and the elected. To claim, therefore, that any great formal extension of industrial democracy in the middle ranges of the industrial hierarchy would greatly diminish our problems is to misunderstand the nature of labour relations entirely.

Nevertheless, there is a good deal to be said for increasing the scope and the practice of participation at the extremes of the industrial spectrum —
  (a)   at the level of government *and*
  (b)   at the level of the workshop.
The establishment of the NEDC by Selwyn Lloyd in 1962 was an early recognition of the need for discussions on the problems of the economy and of its direction. Much good work has been done by the Office and the meetings of the Council have undoubtedly been fruitful in establishing valuable relationships between the individual members. But this is hardly enough and there is a need for the practice

22

to be extended and widened — the tripartite discussions at Downing Street and Chequers in the last two years are a valuable pointer to this need. The TUC and the CBI have a standing and a responsibility in the community that requires and deserves consultation. An on-going dialogue about the nature of the social and economic problem is, therefore, essential.

A reconstituted NEDC would need to meet more frequently and might usefully include one or two economists and other relevant academics. It would also have an agenda that in theory included *any* item raised by individual members or by the different parties to the Council. At the same time, two other conditions need to be satisfied, firstly, that any subject debated by the Council must be considered in its entirety and not merely in isolation from other subjects. For example, the adequacy of state pensions must be related to the priorities given to other items in the socio-economic package. Should increases in pensions have a higher rating in any one year than increases in earned incomes? Or can the economy sustain both? If not, will it be necessary to modify previous policies with respect to growth and thus threaten the maintenance of full employment? Equally, what are the elements that contribute to the overall aim of higher growth?

And what factors tend to frustrate its progress? The agenda could include debates on all aspects of industrial relations.

Discussions of this sort that begin the process of thinking about the unthinkable would do much to remove some of the preconceived notions about the operation of the economy and about the legitimate aspirations of the work-force. But to achieve maximum impact there is much to be said for devising some means of ensuring that the widest publicity should attend the discussions. It would be worth considering whether a public gallery should be introduced or alternatively whether NEDC should be empowered to take TV time for the purpose of informing the public. If this latter suggestion is worthwhile it would need to be objectively screened but without the needling and destructive obsession that some TV producers appear to have with 'failure' and 'conflict'. It will be argued by the media men that such presentations will have no news value. But we do not have to accept the view of those who see 'current affairs' in terms of studio brawls or that the public is so moronic that it will not spare some time to hear about its own problems.

The second area where participation demands imaginative development is at the other extreme — the workshop. The term 'workshop' is used generically to describe the interface between labour itself and the first levels of management. — the shop-floor, the office, the station. It is here that the most profound improvement in attitudes and involvement can be expected from the use of enlightened management techniques.

Management's primary duty is to be efficient at all levels and particularly so in the interests of the managed. Mere goodwill is not enough, for 'management' is a task that engages the mind as well as heart. It is an activity that requires clear heads as well as kind hearts. Efficiency is a long-term exercise, and the tragedy of much managerial planning lies in the slaying of a beautiful scheme by an ugly short-term fact. And that ugly fact is quite often the independence of people. Thus 'efficiency' seen in short-term considerations only is frequently frustrated by a work-force that has been previously alienated.

Management needs to understand the complex of reasons that motivate people. What makes the worker tick? Why do people behave as they do? How can we unleash the will to work in people who are not inherently lazy? What inhibits a greater regard for higher standards of social responsibility? The answers to these questions lie in the attitudes of management to its employees. In general terms, we are told, there are two groups of managers. One group thinks of workpeople as indolent, lacking in ambition, abhorring responsibility, inherently self-centred, resistant to change, gullible, and the easy dupes of charlatans and demagogues. A second group of managers has confidence in subordinates, has a willingness to delegate, sets challenging goals for themselves as well as others, is considerate of subordinates' feelings, involves workpeople in decision-making as far as they are able and is honest and open with them.

The second group's attitude is the more appropriate. Workpeople

24

will tend, like the rest of us, to conform to the image we have of them and we ought, by now, to have rejected that injunction to management of 'speak softly but carry a big stick'. The problems of human relationships, at that point where the work is done, do not flow from instinctive human faults but much more from the nature of industrial organisation and from management philosophy and practices. A more benign management view would seek to enlarge the areas of joint regulation and responsibility at the shop-floor level. And it makes so much sense in terms of efficiency as well as in terms of human relationships. No one knows more about the job than the men who actually do it. This is a truism of labour relations that has been demonstrated more frequently than not when the best-laid plans of efficiency experts have been overtaken by the men themselves. It is almost an occupational 'hazard' for 'time-study' men to have their carefully prepared schemes beaten by workmen who always seem to find another better way of doing the job.

There is a deep well of talent, ingenuity and of good will at the lower levels that can be tapped, for the benefit of all — if we have the wit and the imagination to do so.

iii. The Relationship Between Size and Conflict

My final area of new thinking poses the problem of 'size in industry' as a factor in alienation. I believe that, in the field of human behaviour in industry, we try to regulate relationships on too large a scale. There is a natural 'groupiness' about people. People like to belong and to work in groups and they like those groups to be small. Yet in the world of management and of industry we are obsessed with size. Because 'bigness' as such may be appropriate to the intensive production of consumer goods, we then automatically apply the same concept to the organisation of men — in the fatuous belief that men will ignore their inborn and instinctive tendencies and give to some mammoth corporation the loyalty they give to their natural group. People have a hierarchy of loyalties that always moves upward from the smaller to the larger.

The smaller group loyalty is always the strongest, and it can only

25

temporarily be displaced when the larger allegiance is challenged by
another similar, but external grouping. Thus one's form at school
is the best form and will be defended against the rest of the school.
This is also true whether the basic unit is one's college in a
university, unit in the army; branch in a trade union – each is more
important to the member than the larger grouping of which it is a
part. Yet we so often seem to ignore this truth.

Is it conceivable and possible that we can organise industry in
such a way, that reserves to bigness those elements that are
appropriate to the large scale and to the small scale those factors
that are equally appropriate to it? Do we not commit a fundamental
error when we assume that because investment, marketing and
purchasing may all be centralised with advantage – that human
beings will also respond to the same stimulus? Is a policy of
integrated disintegration a feasible one for the structure of industry?
Equally can we not have a technology that releases an interest in
work and maximises the significance of labour, rather than the
reverse?

In the world of industrial organisation and production the factor
of labour is too often the absent factor at the planning stage. When we
plan our mergers and seek ever more opportunities to harvest the
economies of scale through vertical and horizontal integration or
create our disparate conglomerates, at what stage do we consider
the contribution of labour? And when is it fed into the planning?
Is it too much to complain that the primary consideration is how
much we can get rid of, rather than how much we can use? And are
not such policies, in consequence, often self-defeating in the long run?
If we uplift the material standards of working people, if we increase
their sense of independence, if we raise their status and develop
their understanding of events and issues – if we do all these things
as a Society – and then as managers we develop our industry and
work processes, so that the end result is the dehumanisation of work –
are we not then in danger of pursuing two hares up divergent paths
and at the same time?

I must confess here too, to a certain disenchantment with the
work of some social scientists. They seem to have contributed not

26

very much more than just to raise the general level of confusion. Too often they lose their way in the labyrinth of political dogma rather than pursuing their investigations towards that 'neutral truth' which is the goal of more objective scientists. I sometimes wonder whether the methods of enquiry and the systematic approach of the technologist can be employed more directly in the resolution of some of these organisational and human problems. Can we employ technology itself to solve the human problems of technological growth? One feels quite often that when some new rearrangement of industry is formulated in some remote and obscure board-room — an arrangement that can affect the lives of so many people — that if the method of scientific enquiry was pursued towards the identification of the objective truth, that is present in the problem, then not only would the factors of finance, investment, marketing etc., be fed into the equation — but, because objective enquiry must, by definition, include *all* factors affecting the outcome, then we could be certain that the 'forgotten factor' of labour would be considered at a much earlier stage than now. We might also find that our financial, marketing and investment strategies were subject to less frustration and defeat than they are. All of which makes not only economic sense but common sense as well. The trouble, however, is that 'common sense' is so uncommon.

Summary

These personal views attempt to appraise the defects in our system of industrial relations. The arguments developed for coping with these defects are based on the motivation of that 99 per cent of the work-force that I profoundly believe is anxious to be reasonable. The arguments make no suggestions for dealing with those who are concerned with replacing the present political system by a new and different order. Such people raise issues to which the industrial relations specialist, as such, can provide no answer. That answer must be supplied by politicians working through Parliament. My arguments, such as they are, are distilled from a lifetime of experience on both sides of industry. That, of course, does not make them right, but it may

27

make them worth discussing. They stem from belief as well as experience. They rely on a view of 'management' that sees its primary task in creating opportunities, releasing potential, removing obstacles and providing guidance. It may be said that that is a starry-eyed view, but seen against the background of contemporary events and what has not been achieved by other methods, it is for me at least a realistic view of man in his industrial environment.

2. THE SOCIAL CONTRACT

Alan Fisher

The Social Contract in History

I have been asked to consider the arguments for, and the nature of,
the social contract which should underline industrial relations and this
inevitably poses an initial problem of definition; or, to be more precise,
a problem of interpretation. Perhaps I can best illustrate the nature of
this problem by making a brief excursion into history. I confess that I
do this with some diffidence because I am not a historian and much
less am I a political philosopher. Nonetheless, I feel compelled to
undertake the exercise because I think it will help demonstrate some
of the difficulties involved in attempting to relate the social contract
theory to contemporary industrial relations.

As I understand it, the theory of the social contract is,
broadly speaking, a theory of political obligation. Those whose
names are most often associated with the theory — men such as
Hobbes, Locke and Rousseau — attempted to justify political
authority on the grounds of the self-interest of individuals within a
society expressed through a process of rational consent. They set
out to demonstrate the value of organised government by comparing
it with what they chose to call 'the state of nature', a condition
characterised by the absence of government authority. On the basis
of this comparison they drew the conclusion that government
authority should be accepted by reasonable men. They saw the
conditions under which that authority should be accepted
presented in the form of a social contract from which they supposed
the rights and obligations of all members of the society could be
logically deduced.

If we could stop at this point, and transfer these concepts to
present-day industrial relations, our task would be made much
simpler than it really is; and I must add that I suspect that many
of those who expound the theory of a social contract of industrial

29

relations do, in fact, cut short their analogous thinking at this point. However, we all know that the principal social contract theorists of the past — while they achieved a wide measure of agreement on methodology — reached very different conclusions, and it is this which creates part of our difficulty.

Hobbes, for example, constructed his social contract as a justification for the necessity of absolute power for the sovereign in return for a guarantee of personal safety to the subject citizens. Because of this it has been said of Hobbes that while he saw life in a state of nature as 'nasty, brutish and short', life under his social contract would have been 'nasty, brutish but a little longer'.

Locke added another dimension to his social contract. On the premise that property rights were as fundamental to the state of nature as the preservation of life itself, he argued that the social contract of civil government was conditional on the protection of private property. I suppose that one could say that Locke was the original suburbanite owner-occupier.

Finally, we have Rousseau, who was a continental European and therefore likely to be more revolutionary in his approach than Hobbes or Locke. He saw the social contract as a combination of men who in the state of nature were timid pacifists and as a consequence he emphasised the element of mutual advantage and consent in his social contract. It was Rousseau who conceived the idea of what he called the 'general will'; we can therefore say that he was the grandfather of that rather nebulous phrase 'the national interest' which we all find alternatively convenient or infuriating — depending on whether it is used for us or against us.

I will readily admit that my interpretation of these widely differing conclusions is subjective. But I hope that when you have made allowances for that you will agree that what I have said demonstrates that the application of the theory of the social contract to industrial relations is by no means the easy task we are sometimes led to believe by those innocents abroad who continually seek a simple panacea to the complex problem of modern industrial society. To strengthen my argument, may I add a further point which I hope will create the honest doubt of enquiry in the minds of those who so far remain unconvinced.

It is fairly easy to establish that, because the social contract theorists differed widely in their conclusions, it is not possible to take any one set of those conclusions and apply them to our present-day problems in the naive belief that we could produce a totally acceptable answer. As part of the same process it is equally important to remember that the motives which prompted the philosophising of the early social contract theorists must also be opened to examination and question. Some historians have argued, for example, that one of the major factors which prompted a concentration of interest in the social contract in the seventeenth and eighteenth centuries was the need to find a new rationale for a society in which expanding mercantile capitalism was struggling to remove the restrictive fetters of feudalism: that it was the need to present a theoretical justification of the material demands of a society in flux which motivated them.

Nor must we overlook the fact that England at that time had passed through a traumatic period in which the king's neck had felt the sharp edge of the executioner's axe and Cromwell's short-lived Commonwealth had been replaced by a refurbished monarchy: a situation in which an abstract theory of social contract might well have brought some measure of comfort to a distressed society, regardless of how unrelated to reality that theory was.

If we like to go further back in history, it can be argued that exponents of the social contract prior to the seventeenth and eighteenth centuries had extremely questionable motives for developing their theories. The medieval clerics, for example, saw in the social contract a method of handing authority to secular government while at the same time imposing limits on that government to guarantee the rights of the church. As one writer put it, the theory of the social contract was 'first hatched in the schools, and fostered by all succeeding papists for good divinity'.

What conclusions can be drawn from history? Basically, I hope to have dispelled the belief that there is some absolutist theory of industrial relations, rooted in the old concepts of a social contract, which if applied on a national scale will find total acceptance and thus eliminate conflict. Each social contract theorist of the past

31

began with his own fixed premise about the state of nature; he was influenced by the material conditions of then existing society and his subjective interest in that society. Ultimately he drew conclusions based on the kind of society for which he had a personal preference.

We must remember that exactly the same factors will influence each one of us when we discuss a form of social contract which we think may be applicable to industrial relations. We are not embarking on an intellectual exploration with unanimity of purpose; we are all partisans with views which reflect our roles in society and our attitudes to society. In short, we have all the ingredients for a lively clash of ideas — and anyone who does not relish that prospect might like to take the opportunity of this natural break to opt out of the proceedings now.

Developments in Government–Trade Union Relations

I will now return from my brief historical journey into political theory to pose a question which I consider to be fundamental to the subject under discussion: Why is it that today, in the latter years of the twentieth century when men are circumnavigating the moon, there is an awakening of interest in the theory of the social contract which has been of little more than academic interest since the eighteenth century? While you are pondering on that question, let me advance a few tentative ideas of my own. If, as I have suggested, the earlier theories of the social contract were an attempt to establish and justify certain social relationships, the current interest may well arise from a belated recognition that during the present century new social forces have arisen which to many people remain unexplained and unjustified and which, as a consequence, they fear as uncontrollable.

Let me put it more precisely. The search for a new interpretation of the social contract specifically related to industrial relations appears to signify an unstated acceptance of the fact that in a complex industrial society, such as ours, the primary social power is to be found at the point of production — in the workplace. And, as a corollary of this, there is a growing recognition that it is largely the relationships which grow out of this point which determine much

32

wider social relationships and can ultimately determine the nature of society in total. Perhaps I can best explore these ideas by using the method of modern historicism which, in contrast to the social contract theorists, endeavours to explain social relationships by taking specific institutions, examining the circumstances of their origins and tracing their subsequent developments.

If the trade union movement had its own Book of Genesis it would undoubtedly open with the words: 'In the beginning there was the man, and the man was an employed person.' I use the phrase employed person not because I am reluctant to use the more emotive description 'worker' nor because I am addicted to the jargon of industrial relations; I use it because in an industrial society, and it is with such a society that trade union history begins, 'employed person' defines somebody with a particular function.

Our original employed person was dependent on someone else — the employer — for his income and he had little or no individual power of decision. He stood in a contractual relationship with his employer which reflected the unequal strength of the two parties. What equality existed in law referred only to the observance of the contract, not to the terms of the contract or the procedure by which it was made. The nature of this contractual relationship between employee and employer was — and remains — the historical justification for trade unions. Trade unions originated with fairly limited objectives: to attempt to redress the inequality between employee and employer by interfering with market forces and tilting the balance a little more towards the employee. They sought to do this by the simple expedient of substituting the collective for the individual, and in doing so they provoked a response by employers and State which led to the chain reaction of events which is still explosively in progress.

It is not without significance that if one looks back at the history of the trade union movement throughout the nineteenth and early part of the twentieth century the high peaks that stand out are not so much the records of strikes over wages or conditions, but rather the conflicts of the unions with the State — by which I mean the government or the courts — over their primary rights to exist and to function effectively.

33

As a digression, but to illustrate my point, it is interesting to recall —
particularly against the background of contemporary events — how the
actions of the State in this direction were often counterproductive and
had the opposite effect to that intended; they helped to create the
circumstances which led to a strengthening of the trade union
movement, both in organisational form and the scope of its powers.
Prior to 1868, for example, there had been frequent attempts by some
trade unionists to construct a national body which would unite all
trade unions in pursuit of a common purpose. These had foundered
primarily because of the sectional rivalries which characterised the
still limited horizons of those men who at that time occupied the
dominant positions in the most influential unions. But when the
Government set up a Royal Commission in 1867, in what was clearly
an attempt to mobilise the support of the 'respectable middle classes'
against trade unions, the effect was to diminish the importance
of sectional rivalries amongst the unions and to create a unanimity of
purpose which made possible the establishment of the Trades Union
Congress and thus provided the focal point necessary for a new stage
of trade union development.

An even more ironic example of the counterproductive efforts
of the State to inhibit the growth of trade union influence can be seen
in the sequence of efforts surrounding the formation of the
Labour Party. Contrary to popular mythology, the leaders of the
TUC in its early years were not bursting at the trouser seams for
social revolution. Indeed, in 1895 the TUC had amended its
Standing Orders, ostensibly to exclude delegates from trades
councils but in fact to prevent 'socialist adventurers', such as Keir
Hardie, from attending the Congress and using it as a propaganda
platform. When, in 1899, the TUC debated a resolution calling for
a conference of unions, co-operative societies and socialist bodies
to 'devise ways and means for the securing of an increased number
of Labour members to the next Parliament' it was opposed by many
of the most important unions, and secured a majority of only
112,000 votes out of the total of nearly one million.

The leadership of the TUC exercised their considerable influence
to limit the practical application of the resolution and when the

34

Laboru Representation Committee was set up in 1900 it attracted the support of only a minority of the unions affiliated to the TUC. Confronted with disinterest on the part of the reluctant midwife, the infant which was later to become the Labour Party may well have perished at birth had it not been for the Taff Vale judgment in the House of Lords a few years later, which secured £23,000 in damages and costs from the Amalgamated Society of Railway Servants and left unions in a position where they had the legal right to strike but where they risked their financial existence if they chose to exercise that right. With a Conservative Government obstinately refusing to introduce legislation which would override the Taff Vale decision and restore the legal protection of union funds, these trade union leaders who had previously opposed direct Labour representation in Parliament became rapid converts to the idea in an attempt to secure the necessary legislative change. By 1906 the number of unions affiliated to the Labour Representation Committee had trebled and in the election of that year it fielded fifty candidates and — to the surprise and horror of employers and their political representatives — secured the election of 29 of them. One of the first acts of the new Liberal Government, despite indignant protests by lawyers and employers, was to push through Parliament the Trade Disputes Act which gave unions immunity from civil action during industrial disputes.

Perhaps I should take this one step further and refer to the Osborne Judgment of the Lords in 1909 which ruled that a trade union, even if its rules gave it the explicit right, could not spend its funds on political objects. Trade unions saw this as the lawyers taking their revenge for the 1906 Trade Disputes Act and at the same time aiming a blow at the newly established Labour Party. The result was that many trade unionists, frustrated by the obstruction of their efforts in Parliament, diverted their political activities to the industrial scene and absorbed the syndicalist theory of 'direct action' which was then being advocated by sections of the movement. It was in part a consequence of this situation that between 1906 and 1913 the number of working days lost in industrial disputes rose to more than 82 million, a figure which makes today's industrial

35

scene look like a sea of tranquillity. To mollify the unions the Liberal Government, with the Home Secretary Winston Churchill acting as its chief advocate, passed the 1913 Trade Union Act which, with limitations, restored the right of unions to spend their funds for political purposes and thus provide themselves with a political base in Parliament.

I have dealt with these related episodes in some detail because I think they are a valuable illustration of a period in history when the State, in its attempts to restrict the development of trade unionism, failed to understand either the social forces at work or the environmental circumstances which generated those forces. As a result it reacted in a way which reinforced the determination of the unions and in the long run enabled them to strengthen their position in society. It is, I think, an illustration which is not without some significance in the present situation.

It is interesting to speculate on what the outcome may have been had the trend set in the late nineteenth and early twentieth centuries continued to develop; but the intervention of the First World War introduced a new element and a corresponding change of attitude on the part of government, employers and the trade union leadership. The collaboration and cooperation engendered by that war became institutionalised with, for example, the creation of the Ministry of Labour in 1917 and the establishement of Joint Industrial Councils and the arbitration machinery of the Industrial Courts Act arising out of the Whitley Committee set up by the Government in 1916, in an endeavour to introduce a more pacific climate in industrial relations. It can therefore be argued, with justification, that the First World War marked a significant turning point in industrial relations. At the same time, however, care must be taken not to over-emphasise the nature of this development. Neither the employers nor the Government had been converted to a pro-union attitude; but they had accepted, as a reluctant fact of life, that the unions could not be legislated into non-effectiveness nor could they be ignored. The only alternative open to the Government was to reach some minimal point of accommodation with the unions in the hopes that such an act of recognition would instil a new sense of responsibility in the unions and strengthen the position of what today would be referred to as the 'moderate' elements.

This policy, with occasional aberrations such as the 1926 General Strike, characterised industrial relations throughout the inter-war period. It was basically a policy of containment, designed to permit the unions to have some degree of institutionalised influence in both industrial relations and national affairs but to put extremely tight limits on the extent of that influence.

It was not until the Second World War that a new stage of development in industrial relations was introduced, but when it came its effects were even more profound than those prompted by the First World War. With the virtual conscription of Ernest Bevin, probably the most influential trade unionist of that time, to the Cabinet as Minister of Labour a direct link was established between the Coalition Government and the TUC. Formally and informally the TUC and its affiliated unions became deeply involved in the affairs of government — which had themselves become extended out of wartime necessity — and they were able to exercise considerable influence on the industrial, economic and social policies of the Government. Indeed, the collaboration between the Government and the TUC General Council on legislative and administrative matters before they were debated in Parliament became so close that on a number of occasions backbench Labour MPs, notably Aneurin Bevan, protested that the sovereignty of the House was being placed in jeopardy and that the constitutional function of MPs was being undermined.

At the other end of the spectrum, in the workshops, thousands of shop stewards and other union representatives were faced with the novel experience of being invited — through joint production committees — to deal with matters which had previously been strictly prescribed as managerial prerogatives. The confidence created in trade unionists by their ability to meet with demands generated by their wartime roles undoubtedly contributed greatly to the enthusiasm which, in 1944, led the TUC General Council, acting on a proposal from my own Union, to prepare an extensive document, with the rather pedestrian title of 'Interim Report on Post-War Reconstruction', which set out in detail the trade union movement's

37

proposals on how Britain's economy and industry should be organised, managed and controlled, when the war had ended. It was undoubtedly the most ambitious and effectively constructed projection of trade union objectives ever produced by the TUC until that time; slogans were translated into concrete proposals with little loss of radical content in the process.

Coinciding with the TUC's excursion into post-war planning, the Government itself engaged in some forward thinking when, in 1944, it published a White Paper on 'Employment Policy'. Basically an application of Keynesian economics to post-war problems, it hesitantly accepted that private enterprise − if left to its own devices − would produce unemployment. It therefore acknowledged that it was the duty of government to pursue policies which would sustain a high and stable level of employment.

These two events, not entirely unrelated, were recognised as significant at the time; but few people, if any, then recognised that they marked the initial development of attitudes which are at the centre of our present-day situation.

For the trade unions, 1944 was the year when they began to move to an effective active role in economic and industrial affairs: they seriously began to construct and present alternative policies designed to achieve social objectives. During the same year the Government formally embarked on a policy which led to the ultimate conclusion that *laissez faire* could not provide the full employment on which economic expansion must be based and it was therefore a legitimate function of government to intervene directly in industrial and common affairs. The role of these two institutions, government and the trade union movement, had therefore reached a point of qualitative change. Inevitably, this would affect their relationships with each other and their relationships with employers and management. The broad scene was therefore set for the development of the pattern of post-war industrial relations.

The Current Significance of the Social Contract

At this point some of you may be questioning why my main emphasis has been on the historical development of relations between government and trade unions when the subject under discussion is the nature of the social contract which should underlie industrial relations. You may feel this is primarily a matter for management and unions but my reasoning is simply this: I am convinced that the decisive factor in determining the basic nature of industrial relations has been the way in which the relationships between government and unions have developed since the turn of the century, to culminate in the present situation in which both government and unions have adopted roles in industrial, economic and social affairs which are markedly different from those they had fifty or so years ago.

I will go further and say that so far as I can see there is no evidence to suggest that this trend will not continue in the future; in fact all the evidence points to a continuing strengthening of the trend. However much some people may dislike the fact, and they are to be found in greater or lesser degree on both sides of industry, the frame of reference for industrial relations is no longer solely a matter for agreement between union and employers; government will play an increasingly decisive role in matters which are of fundamental concern to all who are engaged in industrial relations. This means, in case it has escaped your notice, that political considerations – in the widest possible sense – are, and will continue to be, a built-in factor of industrial relations. There are, I know, many people who are involved in industrial relations who will vigorously deny this and who will argue that they, at least, do not allow political considerations to influence their judgement. I will not question the sincerity of their arguments, but I will say that they are deluding themselves if they think they can make any significant contributions to contemporary industrial relations without considering the politics of the situation.

To demonstrate my point I will get down to the real nitty-gritty of the contemporary scene and apply my arguments to the problems of income policy as seen from various points of view, for it is in this area that the politics of industrial relations burst out through the seams – regardless of the intentions of those expressing the various views.

In order to preserve the continuity of these lectures I will begin with the views expressed by Sir Leonard Neal when he spoke to you last month. Sir Leonard, if I read him correctly, argued that the system of what he called 'free bargaining' had proved itself incapable of coping with the effects of social, political and economic change. Looking ahead he anticipated that in the long term Britain would adhere to the standards of free enterprise, which he defined as based on rewards for incentive and effort, with an occasional touch of the brake applied by Whitehall regardless of whether there was a Conservative or Labour Government. From this he drew the conclusion that it was in the nature of incomes policies in a free society that they were inevitable but likely to be short-term affairs, and that they would continue to appear in Britain in this form.

As a contribution to the development of a more rational form of wage determination, Sir Leonard suggested the creation of a body of 'independent fact-finders' who would establish the objective facts of a claim which was in his words, 'thought to have significant repercussive possibilities in other important industries' or 'within a large company or industry' and 'the likely effect on prices of the product or services involved by any proposed claim or possible settlement.' He added, however, that none of this would preclude the Government from 'indicating' its concept of the year's norm or the maximum for increases in income. He concluded by conceding that his proposals contained, and again I quote him, 'no suggestions for dealing with those who are concerned with replacing the present political system by a new and different order. Such people raise issues which the industrial relations specialist, as such, can provide no answer. That answer must be provided by politicians working through Parliament.'

Those are the views of one industrial relations practitioner and, if I can gauge by the overall tenor of his lecture, Sir Leonard would argue that as a specialist in the field he is concerned with wage determination simply as an objective economic function and not — despite any contrary impressions I may have gathered from his remarks — with the political considerations inherent in the situation.

Other specialists in the field, however, appear to reach conclusions which are explicit in their recognition of political considerations. I will

quote only one whose pedigree is as impeccable as it is varied: Alex
Jarratt who, as you all know, has played key roles in the Department
of Employment, the National Board for Prices and Incomes and the
CBI. At a conference just two years ago, Alex Jarratt reviewed —
on the basis of his personal involvement — the attempts of the last
Labour Government to introduce a workable incomes policy and he
reached this primary conclusion:

> 'Attempting to apply this view of the past to the future, I think
> there can be no question of reintroducing a formal incomes policy
> in isolation. It has to be part of an overall approach to economic
> and social improvement, to be in some way a positive policy.
> The association with restraint, which people remember very
> clearly, led in part to the death of the last policy. Also it is
> necessary to accept, like it or not, that people's expectations have
> been raised, and raised very rapidly, by successive governments
> and virtually every consumer business in the country.'

This statement, as I interpret it, is a clear recognition by a non-politician
of the basic political considerations involved in any discussions of
incomes policy. It is interesting to note that Lord George-Brown, when
he was a plain 'Mr' and the Secretary of State for Economic Affairs,
used very similar arguments to those of Alex Jarratt — although
expressed in very dissimilar language — when he was addressing a TUC
Conference of union executive committees on the need to accept the
Labour Government's incomes policy in April 1965. He said:

> 'I was always brought up from the very earliest days in the
> trade union movement to believe that in the end we are more than
> wage bargainers. Our people aim higher than the mere satisfaction
> of their basic fodder requirement. Our people want to play a
> higher role in society and take more decisions as citizens, and to
> live in a society of which they can feel proud because it is fair,
> because it is decent, because it is equalitarian. The policies we are
> collectively offering you I believe will help us to make a great, an
> enormous breakthrough in the achievement of the age-old and
> historic aim of our movement.'

It was, of course, as Alex Jarratt implied, the failure of the Government
to make any significant moves towards the realisation of the promises

41

held out to us by George Brown in 1965 that led to the collapse of the Labour Government's incomes policy. This was clearly shown by the tenor of the debate at a further TUC Conference of Executives in 1967 in the same hall in which we had been spellbound by George Brown only a few years before. One speaker summed it up as follows:

'Even allowing for our scepticism, the events of the last two years have left us disturbed, disappointed and dismayed with the apparent inability of the Government to cope with the problems of external finance, its failure to promote economic growth and its predilection for placing almost total responsibility for the country's economic difficulties on the pay packets of the workers . . . time and again our expectations have been frustrated.'

The speaker, incidentally, was Alan Fisher — then Assistant General Secretary of NUPE. But I must hasten to point out that I was not alone in my attitude for the TUC General Council — of which I was not then a member — was even more explicit in its report to the conference. The report is worth quoting because it does, in fact, provide one of the foundation stones which trade unions will insist must be included in any attempts to construct a social contract of industrial relations involving an incomes policy.

'Trade unionists are not interested in an incomes policy which is based on the assumption that the share of the national income going to working people will remain the same. Their interest lies in a radical and progressive incomes policy which will increase their share in the nation's wealth. Nor do the General Council accept it as axiomatic that, if some working people can get more than some predetermined norm, it follows automatically that other working people must get less. What trade unionists are concerned about — and Congress has repeatedly made this clear — is that the standards of some people should be pushed forward faster than those of others. The people who should be pushed forward fastest of all are those who by common consent are in the ranks of the low-paid. Those who should be held back are mainly to be found in the ranks of the top ten per cent of the population who receive at least twenty-five per cent (and

42

almost certainly a good deal more) of the nation's income, including all non-wage incomes. These people have not been notably affected by incomes policy as it has operated so far. It is for the Government to identify these people, about whom there is much less information available than about wage-earners, and to take action which will convince working people that incomes policy has not only an economic purpose but a social justification.'

Three years after that restatement of trade union attitudes towards incomes policy – and three months before the Labour Government was defeated in the General Election – the TUC General Council, in its 1970 Economic Review, was again explicit in setting out views which have considerable significance to anyone talking in terms of a social contract of industrial relations.

'The trade union movement has repeatedly reaffirmed its support for an incomes policy, but has defined with some precision the types of policy that it will and will not accept. It has insisted that such a policy must be part of an overall economic and social policy . . . It has affirmed that the objectives of this overall economic and social policy must be acceptable to trade unionists, and in accord with trade union aims.'

This, I think, returns me to the point of departure in this section: the increasing importance of political factors in the field of industrial relations. Whatever reluctance there may be in some other quarters, the trade union movement recognises that political considerations – *and political action by government* – is a major factor in determining the character of industrial relations. Our argument is not that there should be no government intervention, but what the nature of that intervention should be and what the policy objectives of government are in making that intervention.

Conclusions

I think I have now reached the point where, to facilitate discussion, I must summarise my arguments so far and then conclude by presenting a concise, but precise, outline of the objectives which the trade union movement would want to see included in any agenda for discussions with the government and employers' organisations designed to explore the possibility of constructing what you may choose to call a social contract of industrial relations.

1. I do not believe that any useful purpose can be served by supposing that conflict in industry can be eliminated, or even minimised, by attempting to apply to industrial relations an abstract theory of social contract which may be filled with good intentions but is completely unrelated either to historical experience or to the real alignment of contemporary social forces which have their origin in industry.

2. Historical experience, certainly since the turn of the century, has demonstrated that the determining factor in industrial relations is the relationship between government and unions. This relationship in turn depends, in a large part, on the objectives which governments and unions set for themselves and on how they see their respective roles in pursuing these objectives. Since the end of the war both government and unions have become increasingly concerned with objectives which, while they may not coincide, have created an overlap of interest in critical areas and this has opened up new perspectives throughout the whole range of subjects which are somewhat loosely called industrial relations. Any attempts to develop a social contract of industrial relations must, therefore, rest upon this historical experience and the situation it now presents us with.

3. As much as some people may deplore or dislike it, the fact that relationships between government and unions are a determining factor in industrial relations automatically injects political considerations into industrial relations and in the process extends their subject area. This means that anyone who wants to discuss improvements in industrial relations cannot opt out of a sensitive area by saying that it is a matter for the politicians; such a tactic is contracting out of the social contract before the rough draft has been completed.

These, then, are the three basic points I wish to emphasise in my summary. I am convinced that recognition of them is basic to any

44

meaningful understanding of present-day industrial relations and I am further convinced that acceptance of them is crucial to any considerations of, to quote my brief, 'the nature of the social contract which should underlie industrial relations'. Let me assume, just for a moment, that you all accept these basic points and that we are in business. What, then, you will ask, are the terms which the trade union movement — for its part — would want to see included in such a social contract?

To answer that question I can do no better than refer you to the 186-page memorandum of evidence which the TUC submitted to the Donovan Commission. I am sure that you have all read it — but just to refresh you memories I will recapitulate Part B, Section 2, which, you will recall, set out with some precision ten major trade union objectives:

1. Improved wages and terms of employment relating to hours, holidays and similar fringe benefits.
2. Improved workplace environment; more attention to health, safety and welfare.
3. Full employment as a precondition for rising output and rising real incomes.
4. Security of employment and income in the face of industrial changes.
5. Improved social security in times of accidents, sickness, unemployment and old age.
6. Redistribution of national income and wealth — on which no more need be said.
7. Industrial democracy, an opportunity to intervene in the decision-making process.
8. A voice in government, more intervention in the decision-making process.
9. Improved public and social services, better health and education services, more and better houses, improved public transport.
10. Public control and planning of industry, vital as a means of securing the other objectives.

It will be objected that these ten objectives constitute a shopping list of some magnitude, and that no government could possibly concede

45

to them — regardless of what concessions the unions were prepared to make on their side in order to conclude a social contract which embraced such objectives.

This I would readily accept if they were being advanced as immediate objectives, something which the unions wanted to see established next week or next month; but we have never done this. What we have done, and what we will continue to do, is to seek specific commitments from government that it accepts these objectives — as objectives — and constructs immediate policies which demonstrably work towards them. As the TUC commented in its evidence to the Donovan Commission: 'There can be no absolute distinction between methods and objectives. All these objectives are seen as the means to the good life, which is the ultimate objective in all of them', and that is what a trade unionist would say must be the nature of any social contract which should underlie industrial relations.

3. PARTICIPATION IN UK MANAGEMENT

G.A.H. Cadbury

Introduction

I am honoured to have been asked to take part in the 1974 series
of Stockton Lectures on 'Industrial Relations in a Changing World'.
In discussing my subject, I shall concentrate on participation in the
management of business, although this leaves aside the management
of a wide range of other activities, notably the public services, where
the issues of participation are at least as relevant.

I am conscious that the word participation has been so over-used
that to many it is no more than a catch phrase. The state of the
debate on participation was well summed up by the French labour
leader quoted by Innis Macbeath: 'Everyone is talking and
no one is listening.'[1] My reason for continuing the talk is that I
believe in participation and I see a real danger of participation in
practice not living up to the expectations that have been formed
of it. As Sir Leonard Neal said in the first of these lectures,
participation is being advertised by some 'as the new detergent for
industrial relations'; this can only result in disillusion and in
participation becoming yet another headstone in the cemetery of
discarded business philosophies, before its potential has been
realised.

The point above all that I wish to make in this lecture is that the
road to participation in UK management will be hard and slow and
there is no room for the woolly goodwill and imprecise invocations
which take up so much of the current debate on participation.[2]
I do not draw attention to the obstacles to participation to deter,
but to ensure that a practical and realistic view is taken of its
probable progress in industry and of what it has to offer. Participation
cannot by its nature be imposed. Its advance depends not on
organisational provisions, necessary though they are, but on how
much individuals actively want to participate.

47

To me participation in managing an institution means giving its members a share in the way it is run. I accept that what we are concerned with is the degree of participation in management. No enterprise can be run without participation from the people who make it up; participation is normally exercised through the management line and through whatever system of collective bargaining or consultation obtains. Reference to 'participation' is therefore shorthand for 'a greater degree of participation in management', but it does involve a deliberate change in management methods based on accepting the advantages of the participative approach.

A recent Harvard Business Review article[3] found a surprising degree of unanimity among practising managers about what the apparently ambiguous phrase 'participative leadership' meant.

'Despite the fact that participative leadership is an abstract concept, the managers in the study reached a high level of agreement . . . This high level of agreement suggests that the study managers hold a reasonably clear and uniform understanding in their concrete interpretation of participative leadership.'

Thus, the operational meanings of participative and participation are clear to practising managers. Managers disagree not over what the words mean, but over how, and how far, they should be put into effect. The case for participation in management can be made on moral grounds, along the same lines as the case for a democratic system of politics. An employee who remains with a company throughout his working life depends on it for his earnings, his job satisfaction, his opportunities for advancement and, frequently, a substantial part of his retirement income. An individual with that degree of commitment to a company should have some say in its objectives and how they are to be achieved.

The practical case for participation, from the employee's point of view, rests on the scope it gives him to make fuller use of his abilities and to acquire more control over his working situation. From the employer's angle, participation taps the abilities of more people and of skills and experience complementary to management's

48

professional and technical expertise. Participation should therefore lead to better decisions and more important, to decisions commanding greater commitment.

Both individuals and companies must pay a price for the advantages that participation has to offer. The opportunity for individuals to play a more active role requires acceptance of the responsibilities that this will entail. The company must recognise that decisions will be more difficult to arrive at and that there will be longer-term consequences for its development as an enterprise. There is however considerable backing for the practical effectiveness of participation, as this quotation from Stendenbach confirms —

> 'there exists almost no study which does not show that workers' participation in decision-making promotes work satisfaction and produces other beneficial effects such as better economic performance. This consistency of research results is very rare if not unique in social research. It indicates that participatory systems respond to basic human needs which release otherwise dormant or suppressed energies and capacities.'[4]

Clearly this is a key conclusion. If participation turned out to be no more than an exercise in public relations, it would have little to offer either the company or the individual.

The argument that greater participation in management will buy off more extreme demands should carry little weight. Participation must stand on its own merits. It will be hard enough to introduce backed by the best of motives. Based on anything less it will be self-defeating. My concern is that the movement for greater participation in management is now confused about aims and methods and that it is not facing the inescapable practical problems that must be overcome for it to succeed in our present industrial climate. Nothing will more discredit the participative approach than if companies assume that it can be introduced by passing a Board minute. Its introduction involves accepting a new attitude of mind and seeing its future implications; its implementation depends on training and on making specific

49

changes at all levels in the enterprise's structure and working methods.

The Demand for Participation

To assess realistically the future of participation in management one must first ask why there should be such widespread interest in participation now, not only in industry but also in fields like education and politics. Without weighing them against the wider aims of the movement of which they form part, one cannot assess how far the forms of participation in management currently being discussed are likely to prove of permanent worth.

A basic reason for this interest in participation must be the higher standard of general education, combined with a less intense preoccupation with simply making both ends meet. Those entering industry in the last fifteen years are not only better-educated than their predecessors, but have been educated in a different way; less is taken for granted and more is open to question. Moreover, education has become more closely involved with directly influencing society by establishing courses in the social sciences, applied economics and environmental studies. The educational message is that no systems or organisations need be accepted in their present form and that the individual is responsible for re-shaping them in the light of his own beliefs and experience. Further, the consequences of better communications are that people have become aware of how others live and have been shown what can and is being done in other countries; international standards of comparison have been introduced against which to measure British methods and progress. Expectations are therefore raised. Existing practices and institutions are no longer seen as insuperable obstacles to meeting them.

Education and communications are general forces behind the present interest in participation, but there are others more specific to this country's industrial situation. The outstanding argument for a greater degree of participation in the management of British industry rests on the example of Europe.

The economic success of mainland Europe over the last two decades is unquestioned. This industrial recovery has been accompanied by more statutory encouragement for participation and experiment with organisational forms for promoting it than have occurred here. Without asserting cause and effect, it nevertheless is difficult to argue against greater participation in management when the lesson from Europe and in particular from Germany, is that formal participation and economic growth have gone together.

An argument frequently cited for increasing interest in industrial participation is that job specialisation and simplification have been taken too far: 'the actual processes at work are becoming more repetitive, more monotonous and more frustrating.'[5] I doubt whether work is more repetitive than it was, considering the vigorous attack on work simplification that is to be found in Adam Smith. Mechanisation has by definition eliminated the most automatic movements and the shortest cycle times. However, factory work has become less demanding physically and yet requires continuous concentration without offering much mental stimulus. To this extent, that it cuts people off from establishing and maintaining social relationships, industrial work has become more frustrating. Even so, the change is more in our view of what work should have to offer than in its nature. Certainly, work has become more monotonous in the clerical field. Here the situation is analogous to the earlier days of scientific management in the factory. Changes in technology have made many clerical operations more repetitive and have encouraged the development of larger administrative units; evidence for this is the growth of clerical and administrative unions. The change in the industrial work-force could also have contributed to the increased interest in participation. The proportion of administrative, clerical and technical staff has risen and that of manual workers has fallen, a trend reinforced by the continuing rise in the size of companies, as larger companies tend to have a higher proportion of qualified staff than smaller. Since the priorities of qualified staff are likely to differ from those of manual workers, this change is important not only because it may promote the movement for more participation, but also because it will affect its direction. Again, concern for security and continuity of employment against the background of an increasing number of mergers has grown.

51

This raises a defensive rather than a positive argument for participation which can only be met by participation at the highest level of decision-making. It is a British rather than an European phenomenon. If we go back to 1954, out of 2,126 firms in manufacturing industry (excluding steel) which were then quoted on the Stock Exchange, more than 400 had been acquired by 1960. Not only did merger activity quicken through the 1960s, but also its nature changed through the increasing number of conglomerate and transnational mergers. Those working in a business could find that at relatively short notice they had become part of a larger company which mainly operated in a different field, or that the ownership of their business had been transferred overseas to strangers. One element in the pressure for greater participation in management in this country therefore is the resolve of employees to influence this type of decision more and to ensure that their interests are balanced with the shareholders'. At the same time companies are seen as becoming less responsive to the views of ordinary people, whether employees or consumers, through their size and the divorce of professional management from ownership.

It can be said that in spite of all these arguments in support of participation, pressure for it has come from outside industry and that there is no general demand for it from within. This is on the surface true, although there can be no doubt about the expression of the defensive reaction just referred to. I would argue, on two grounds, that the demand for participation in management is latent, rather than that it does not exist. First, participation is progressive and feeds on itself, so one cannot measure the demand for it until you introduce it; putting the same point negatively, if you were to reduce the degree of participation in an enterprise. I am convinced that there would be a strong reaction. Secondly most managers would agree that the attitude towards authority significantly changed in the last few years; not only is more being questioned, but the range of issues that are being raised is so much wider. This new situation reflects the demand for participation, whether the label is consciously attached to it or not.

52

I shall discuss participation in management under three broad headings; the levels at which participation can take place, the barriers to its introduction in the current UK industrial situation and the issues with which participation may be expected to deal. While much of the analysis is concerned with the problems of participation, it also includes what seem to me the most promising paths of progress. The business background against which I set participation is that of a manufacturing company; the service industries will have differences of emphasis and their own advantages and disadvantages in participative terms.[6]

The Different Levels of Participation

Participation in management can take place at three main levels: the board, the factory or office unit and the shop-floor, by which I mean the level at which the primary manufacturing or clerical operations of the business are carried out.

Attention has inevitably been directed to participation in management at board level, because the board is the senior decision-making body in a company and it is the board that will be affected by the proposals of the draft EEC Fifth Directive. The Fifth Directive, if adopted, would force a common company structure upon public companies. They would be legally required to have three distinct organs — a general assembly of shareholders, a supervisory board and a management board. The management board would run the business; the supervisory board would control the management board and the general assembly would be responsible for shareholder representation on the supervisory board. The Directive's only options concern the manner of appointing the supervisory board; the employees either nominate or elect one-third of the supervisory board or, if the board is self-appointing, employee and shareholder representatives can object to individual appointments.

Participation in management at board level raises more problems than at either of the other two. First, the issue of participation tends to become confused with that of company structure, as it does in the

53

Fifth Directive. The test to be applied to an enterprise's structure is how far it achieves the required balance between the internal responsibility of a company to make the best use of its resources and its external responsibilities to the society in which it operates. Once that balance has been struck, participation can be built in to whatever pattern of organisation emerges. I do not argue that participation may not be important in the reform of company structure, but its introduction need not wait for such reforms and should certainly not be confused with them.

Further, the appointment of employee directors to public company boards in Britain raises a constitutional problem and challenges either the nature of the unitary board or the employee director's position on it. If the employee director is accepted as the representative of a particular set of interests the board's role is changed, since it would now become a negotiating body, a role quite distinct from its collective responsibility for the running of the enterprise. If, however, the board continues with the doctrine of collective responsibility intact, then the employee director has ceased to be an employee director because he is bound by the same considerations as the other board members.

Participation in management at board level is only likely to succeed if it grows out of practical experience in participation at other levels in the organisation. If the movement towards greater participation starts at board level, it will raise the maximum expectations for the minimum results. Second, effective participation at board level is based on a participative structure which extends throughout the enterprise. The top of the pyramid is the wrong end from which to build such a structure. However, the concern expressed earlier about the possibility of major changes in the ownership or nature of a company is real and legitimate and can only be met by providing some participative link with the board. One way to achieve this, which avoids confusing the issue of participation with that of board structure, would be to form a separate participative body at company level, parallel to the board, rather than integrated into it as with employee directors, or superior to it as with the supervisory board. This body would meet with board members regularly and have the right to participate in certain key management decisions like those relating to mergers, closures and investment plans. The Industrial Partnership Association have set out how a body of this kind, which they refer to as an 'advisory board', might be formed and operate:

'The advisory board would meet regularly. It would have no legal powers or responsibilities, but the employee representatives would have similar information made available to them as members of the supervisory board in the EEC type two-tier system. It would have no power to disapprove the main board plans. It would in effect "trade such rights" for the right to meet regularly with key main board members to discuss any matter relating to the present or future of the company.'[7]

The works or site has the longest history of participative management, particularly in Germany where the concept dates back to 1848. Participation in management at works level depends on the acceptance higher in the company of participation as an aim. Given that backing, the mechanics of putting participation into practice are simpler at works rather than board level for several reasons. Most immediate decisions affecting conditions of work and its organisation are taken at this level. Those involved are familiar with operating details and can contribute directly to the unit's work. Problems of representation and communication are manageable, because the numbers involved are not usually too large and everyone works on the same site. In fact, the interesting question is why have not works councils or their collective bargaining equivalents made a greater impact in this country, when structurally this would seem to be the natural level for the development of collective participation?

On the shop floor, the main emphasis in participation has been to give individual employees or groups greater control over their own work situation. Participation here is best known for the contribution it is making to job satisfaction, by allowing the working group to decide how a given task should be organised and allocated between the members of the group. It differs from the other two levels in offering the opportunity for individual as opposed to collective participation.

55

This brief summary shows that participation in management at different levels in the enterprise raises different issues and requires different structures for resolution. Any discussion of participation in general is likely to be unproductive. From the earlier analysis of the motives that lie behind the pressure for increased participation in management, it is clear that they cannot all be satisfied by a single participative body: the need for security will only be met by some participation at board level, while the ordinary employee will obtain more personal satisfaction from his work only by participation in the first level of management. Nevertheless, these different aspects of participative management do hang together. The simplest way of studying their relationship is to see how they work and have evolved in another country — Norway. Norway's experience is instructive because the progress of participation can be followed from the industrial situation at the end of the Second World War and because progress has been backed by thorough research, which gives a lead as to the conditions necessary for participation's successful growth.

Norwegian Experience

Joint production committees were formed in Norway of management and employee representatives, to re-establish the country's economy after the war. From this grew a structure of works councils; the issues dealt with by collective bargaining widened. The result was that the problems of providing people with work that they thought worthwhile were raised in Norway well before they became generally recognised elsewhere.

In the 1960s a research committee jointly sponsored by the employers and the trade unions undertook a series of experiments in participation in the Industrial Democracy Programme. It began by investigating the practical results of putting employee representatives on the boards of nationalised industries. Their findings were that these appointments had been of little value and had not filled the communication gap between the board and the shop-floor. As a result research was switched to how the individual employee could obtain more satisfaction from his work. This led to the establishing of

56

certain standards to which a job had to measure, were individual participation to be encouraged. On the basis of this research, a number of companies went ahead with their own programmes for giving employees more control over their work and more opportunity to work collectively. This experience has led to a swing away from traditional shop-floor organisation to the development of autonomous working groups and to requests for more technical and managerial training, so that the working group could widen its area of influence. While shop-floor participation was thus progressing, a more formal works council structure was also being developed. Managers were obliged to attend regular council meetings, to provide information on sales, production and employment and to notify changes in work or conditions important to employees. Although works councils have remained advisory bodies, their right to be kept fully informed about the financial situation of the business and of anticipated operating changes is clearly defined and has enabled them to participate in management decisions. An interesting further step has been the formation of a Participation Council at national level, made up of representatives from trade unions and employers' associations. The Council promotes the cause of participation by acting as an information and training centre and by furthering research into management-union co-operation.

Finally, the issue of board level participation has been raised again, although it had been dropped earlier because it had been ineffective in practice and was considered not to be the right starting point to extend participation throughout the enterprise. With participation in management established on the shop floor and at works level, there is now understandable pressure for employee representation on the board. Norwegian joint stock companies normally have a unitary board. It has been proposed that all such companies above a certain size should also have a new body, to be called the 'Board of Representatives.' One-third of its members would be elected by and from the employees and two-thirds by the shareholders. The Board would appoint the management board and ratify major policy decisions, so that it will

57

have much in common with a 'European' supervisory board.

A number of relevant points arise from the Norwegian experience, even allowing for the differences in size and industrial background. There is close cooperation between employers and trade unions in the introduction of participation, formalised in the Participation Council. Participation was based on the existing management/labour system of joint working and then extended: research was used to validate the effectiveness of different approaches. The participative structure grew from the roots up, participation at one level reinforcing participation at another. There also was emphasis on training for all having part to play in the participative process. The one sure conclusion that I would draw from this discussion is that no single form of participation in management will meet the needs of all levels in all businesses in this country. Britain needs a period of experiment in which different approaches are tried by a variety of types of enterprise. Even this, however, will not be as useful as it should be, unless the findings from these experiments are collated and communicated by some central body, to undertake the task of research into participative methods and the training required for implementing them. Such a body would also provide the means of involving academic institutions and drawing on their resources.

Barriers to the Introduction of Participation

Barriers to greater participation are not peculiar to this country, but some will be more difficult to overcome in Britain than in the rest of Europe because of the strength of our industrial traditions. The simplest way of discussing these barriers is to consider the impact of a greater degree of participation on managers and on organised labour and then to look at the question of representation, which is central to effective participation.

Clearly, an increased degree of participation in management will directly affect the way in which managers carry out their functions. It will involve changes in managerial methods. The first hurdle therefore to be cleared in introducing it is to convince managers of the need to change their approach and then that the particular change being advocated is the right one. To a professional manager, the only convincing arguments will be that participative management has advantages for managers and those they manage and that it has been shown to work in practice. If these arguments are right companies moving towards a greater degree of participation in management will have a competitive edge in recruitment at all levels. Managers will reflect the same general pressures for participation as other members of society. They will see in the growth of participative management the opportunity for many to overcome the frustrations of their own jobs. Indeed, managers could reasonably expect a commitment to the spread of participation throughout the management hierarchy to be a condition to introducing it at any one level.

I do not underestimate the barrier that a change in managerial methods represents, even though management's function is to be dissatisfied with the existing situation and be determined to improve it. The change called for by more participation in management is particularly difficult to achieve, since it involves a change in outlook and attitude. A manager may be intellectually convinced of the need and believe that he has made a change, without it having worked through to his managerial reflexes. The basis of the change must be a genuine intention to adopt a new management approach, because of what it offers.

Frederick Chaney and Kenneth Teel have described their experience over four years of introducing participative management into a factory at supervisory level.[8] Their conclusion was:

'Participative management offers no simple, easy solution to all organisational problems; for managers and supervisors who are willing to work hard at it, however, it does offer high probabilities of pay-off in both increased production and improved employee attitudes. Participative management is a practical way of integrating individual and organisational goals. It gives employees opportunities to play active roles in planning, coordinating and controlling their own work and thus makes employees' work more meaningful and relevant.'

I would support introducing participation at the level of the

59

supervisor, as this is the logical starting place if the introduction is backed by the employees concerned and senior management.

The impact is direct. The supervisor's job changes from ensuring that each employee correctly fulfils his allotted task to enabling the working group to cooperate effectively in meeting agreed targets. In effect the supervisor's role becomes less authoritarian and more supportive. An insecure or inadequately trained supervisor cannot do this. It will not suit the natural management style of all supervisors. Inevitably some supervisors will see participation as reducing their authority and improving the status of the shop-floor worker at their expense, at a time when they are increasingly becoming organised to maintain their managerial position. Therefore, the choice of starting point is sensitive. Both individual supervisors and their collective representatives must be convinced that it is soundly chosen.

Supervisors will also recognise that participative management not only involves fundamental change, but also makes management's task harder. It can therefore only follow training specifically designed to prepare for the change. The task is harder because one of the fundamental misconceptions about participation is that it will lead to unanimity. Faced with a decision, the members of a working group are likely to put forward several different proposals and, while the commitment of those whose ideas are to be adopted may be taken for granted, commitment also has to be won from those whose views have been discarded.

'True participative management requires that the supervisor works closely and actively with his employees to plan, organise, coordinate and control the work of the group. The supervisor shares his responsibilities with the group — he does not surrender them.'[9]

To equate participative management with permissive management is to misunderstand the challenge that it presents and its demand to handle conflict constructively. Managers will have no difficulty over participation in times of growth, of success and of common purpose. They will also have to persevere with it in the face of failure, and of divided counsels passionately held.

An increased degree of participation in management also affects

company organisation. The traditional organisation of a firm starts
with the objectives of the enterprise, set by the board; individual
management positions are then defined by their part in meeting
those objectives. All jobs below board level derive their existence,
limits and authority from the objective setting function of the
board. The introduction of participation alters this theoretical pattern.
In particular, participation at board level means that the definition
of the aims of the business becomes circular, with the board being
prepared to modify its original aims in the light of participative
discussions. The practical point arises that if the managerial approach
changes, then parallel changes must be made in the organisation.
It will have to adapt to a redirection of the flow of information, to
a changed pattern of decision-making and to a new time cycle. These
changes will affect the level of staffing and the links between staff.
The more rigid a   management hierarchy and decision-making
process an organisation has, the more it will be changed by a greater
degree of participation in management. An organisation that
uses project teams drawn from different functions and different
levels of management can move towards a greater degree of
participation relatively easily, since the approach has already been
organisationally accepted.

To sum up, there is practical managerial evidence to support the
introduction of participative management, but its introduction involves
a basic change in attitudes and methods. The magnitude of that change
must be appreciated, as must the degree of commitment required to
sustain it. The critical level of management for participation is
supervisory, since this is the main point of contact between the
company and the employees, but it is at this level that the threat to the
existing pattern of authority will seem most real.

Organised Labour

Increased participation faces trade unions with greater difficulties than
it does managers, and it does not call forth the same degree of self-
interest to overcome them. There is first the ideological obstacle that a
part of the trade union movement rejects participation in an economic

61

system it seeks to change. Rule 3 of the National Union of Mineworkers, for example, sets out the objective of joining 'with other organisations for the purpose and with a view to the complete abolition of capitalism'. The TUC interim report on Industrial Democracy comments – 'The traditional British trade union attitude to schemes for participation in management of private industry has been one of opposition.'[10] While it is arguable how great this obstacle is in practice, it must leave local officials and ordinary trade union members in some uncertainty about the attitude they ought to take towards participation in management. Significantly, in France similar political objections have meant that only the Force Ouvrière, the smallest of the three national trade union bodies, supports formal participation.

The major obstacle, however, to trade union involvement in participation is the British trade union movement's historical structure. There are currently 466 trade unions, of which 87 have more than 10,000 members. Apart from a minority of industrial unions they are organised by the work their members do. The relationship between a craft union and its members has its roots in common training and the possession of common skills; the primary link is by type of work rather than by its purpose. Its organisation could be described as vertical, in contrast to the horizontal way in which a company organises its work.
The employer's view of an organisation is related to its task; he does not see the business as being divided by skills, but as comprising people linked together by the unit in which they work. These are materially different concepts of organisation of a working group.

On the shop-floor, participation has centred on the problems raised by car assembly lines and on ways of altering the work flow to let groups of employees be responsible for making complete units. This does not normally raise inter-union problems, but a more common work situation is forming and packaging consumer goods. There is little scope for building up this kind of job like the group assembling complete engines, because the forming and packaging operations are in themselves relatively simple, except by increasing

62

operators' responsibility for the setting, running and maintaining of their machines. From a management point of view, this approach is straightforward, since these operations would be seen as a logical production entity. Craft unions, to whom those who normally serviced those machines belong, would view it very differently. Instead of redistributing work among the same group, as in engine assembly, members of a general union would be increasing the range and interest of their jobs by taking work away from craft unions. This method of providing more job autonomy and opportunity to process workers has therefore only made headway in countries having an industrial trade union structure. Yet it is the logical way of making this type of routine work more interesting. It worked in practice during the Second World War when job restrictions were dropped. It parallels the increasing familiarity with technical servicing we all must acquire in the home. Introducing participation at shop-floor level is therefore likely to result in pressure from employees to extend their skills and range of work in ways cutting across existing union boundaries.

Nevertheless, the shop-floor still seems to me the best point of entry for participative management. Here the greatest community of interest lies, since the group concerned already work together on a common task at the same place and will know how their own jobs can be improved. Participation in management on the shop-floor is more of an individual and less of a collective concern and so is more capable of adapting to local circumstances: obstacles are therefore easier to overcome than at the institutional levels of participation. While there will be real problems given present trade union organisation, if the members see advantages in shop-floor participation, it will, in the end, be reflected in the policies and structure of the trade union movement. It is likely to be one force working for an industrial basis of trade union organisation and for reducing the number of unions.

Works councils could have been expected to develop from the joint production committees set up during the two world wars. The reasons that they did not are, presumably, because works councils were not taken seriously enough by employers, who did not give them real responsibility, and because the trade unions, which were stronger than their European counterparts, saw works councils as competing with unionised collective bargaining. This is reflected in the reference to works councils in the TUC Interim Report on Industrial Democracy:

> 'An attempt to introduce a general system of works councils in British industry would lead to one of two things. Either they would duplicate existing structures at plant level, in which case Works Councils would clearly be superfluous: or they would displace and supersede existing trade union arrangements; this latter approach would be even more unacceptable to the trade union movement.'

The fact that the statement is not strictly accurate only emphasises the difficulties facing trade unions in assessing impartially the potential role of works councils. The statement is not strictly accurate because, without a works council, there is no 'existing structure at plant level', meaning a single body, representing all groups of employees at one site. A works council's unique contribution is to take a view on matters that affect the whole working community. This is precisely what the normal machinery of collective bargaining cannot do for two main reasons. First, it does not represent all groups, notably management, and secondly, in a multi-union factory it is not usual for all the unions involved to co-ordinate their approach through one collective bargaining body.

The other half of the TUC statement expresses the fear that works councils would threaten to displace or supersede existing trade union arrangements. The experience of works councils in this country and in Germany does not support this. The dual structure of councils and collective bargaining has proved to be mutually reinforcing, probably because, whether membership of a trade union is required or not, those active in the trade union movement are the natural candidates for election to the works council. This reflects our own company experience, and Innis Macbeath comments that nine out of ten members of German works councils are union members, who number only three out of ten of all workers. Employers would have no interest in forming works councils if they were in fact likely to 'displace or supersede existing trade union arrangements', as there could be no worse industrial relations situation than to have two rival forms of representation. If works councils are extended, a considerable degree of common membership between works councillors and trade union representatives would be natural, which is not to say that works councils and collective bargaining are straight alternatives. The ideological objection could also be raised to works councils, since most European works councils have, as one aim, to further the enterprise's objectives. [11] However, the TUC told the Donovan Commission that participation was in order provided that it respected the boundaries between negotiable issues and managerial issues:

> '... a distinction needs therefore to be drawn between the negotiating function of the employer and the overall task of management. Once this distinction is established, it can be seen that it does not detract from the independence of trade unions for trade union representatives to participate in the affairs of management concerned with production, until the step is reached when any of the subjects became negotiable questions as between trade unions and employers.' [12]

I would argue that this policy enables works councils and collective bargaining bodies to coexist usefully, with issues passing from the former to the latter when 'the step is reached'.

Participation at works level raises no trade union objections, provided that it extends collective bargaining, but my argument is that present methods of collective bargaining do not meet the test of effective participation. Works councils should be extended, because their constituencies comprise everyone working at a particular location, so giving them a natural community of interest. I realise, however, that they cut across the way in which most trade unions are organised; the trade union links together those who do the same type of work, not those who work together. The interests it represents are limited to those of the particular class of employee. An existing works council will also have developed its role over time and established confidence and trust. Setting up a works council is quite a different matter. It raises all the difficulties that have to be faced over the introduction of any new institution in those circumstances. First, it is impossible to predict precisely how a new institution will work. Institutions grow and develop in ways which their founders cannot always foresee. Second, some at least of its work will be being carried out by other individuals or bodies, who will naturally resent the transfer of power.

I shall not discuss in detail the obstacles to trade union participation at board level. The TUC interim report supports the formation of supervisory boards provided that they 'should be the supreme body of the company able to overrule both the board of management and the AGM of shareholders or owners on major decisions.' This recommendation follows a perceptive analysis of the sources of power in a company, but to demand the effective disenfranchisement of the owners of public companies as the price of supporting board participation is hardly to make a realistic offer of support. I have spent time on the problems facing trade unions over participation in management, because participation in Britain can only be developed with their backing. The difficulties winning that support must be faced. This is why participation needs to take advantage of any openings at any level in any company and why progress must be expected to be limited. It would help if the trade union movement's ideological position about participation was clarified, but two basic pressures could involve the trade unions more positively in moves towards greater participation. First, there is likely to be support for more participation from among the membership, particularly on the shop-floor. Second, participation requires an organised structure of representation to be built up. This must be in established trade unions' interests, because once a substantial structure exists it will be easier for them to recruit new members from those who are not at present members.

Representation

The problems of participation become more acute higher up

the company hierarchy, because participation increasingly depends on a formal structure of representation. The basic issue is to ensure that all employees have an equal opportunity to participate. Here again there is a difference in outlook between the company, which has a duty to everyone working in the enterprise, and a trade union, whose concern is its own members. This difference is apparent in the absence of discussion on how employees working outside this country should have their interests represented, under proposals put forward for the appointment of employee directors to the boards of UK public companies. This point does not seem to have been considered in Europe either, presumably because when participation was introduced only a small proportion of the work-force of the companies concerned were employed outside the company's country of incorporation. The British situation reflects the different historical and economic forces shaping the development particularly of the larger UK companies, which are often best placed to introduce participation. If a company has, say, half of its employees abroad, then any discussion of participation at board level which leaves out of account how their views are to be heard must be incomplete. Another issue is how employees who are not members of trade unions are to be represented. Just over one-half of the employed population are not members. An equitable scheme for participation must enable their views to be made known. The problem for manufacturing industry is more limited than those figures might suggest, as the proportion of unorganised employees is low compared with the service industries. In turn, the non-unionised service sector tends to be organised in small units, where the potential for informal participation is highest.

An important aspect of the same issue is managers' position in the representative structure, as their attitude is crucial to the successful introduction of more participation. One criticism of joint consultation in Britain is that far too often it bypasses middle and supervisory management; it is also a weakness of the German works councils that managerial representation is limited. For effectiveness and equity, managers should be fully involved in participation. Effectiveness is measured by the contribution that managers can make to participative discussion and decisions from their training and background knowledge of the company: until training for participation is really under way managers will be the main source of this necessary experience. The equity argument is clear enough, but meeting it is a practical question of how managers in this country have been represented in the past and wish to be represented in future. Managers are seldom collectively represented in manufacturing industry, but it is broadly true that where junior managers are organised it is on traditional trade union lines, while middle managers are more often represented by internal company associations and senior managers rarely have any formal organisation to represent them. The pressure on managers to form representative bodies will grow with the need for them to protect their position in an increasingly insecure and rapidly changing world and to prevent the relative erosion of their terms and conditions of employment.[13]

Apart from protecting their position in this sense, the traditional collective bargaining approach only meets the needs of managers to a limited extent, partly because the manager is concerned with the development of his individual career, which is not a collective issue, and partly because managers, particularly at the more senior levels, value their independent ability to influence events, rather than relying on negotiation. A further complication is the power of professional associations in this country compared with their counterparts in Europe. Membership of a professional association may determine a manager's standing in his own eyes and give him a closer relationship with his fellows outside the company than with his fellow managers in it. Its organisational form parallels that of a craft union.

The future progress of managers' organisations will reflect the conflict between managers' desire to retain their individual relationship with their employer and their need to combine to defend their position in the company. I expect the straightforward union type of organisation to extend upwards, internal management associations to become more independent and demanding and professional associations to involve themselves more in their members' careers. Greater collective organisation will reinforce managers' claim to participate and make it administratively more straightforward. Managers will be particularly concerned to have more of a voice in setting the objectives of their company, a logical consequence of introducing more participation. If on the shop-floor managers are to rely less on hierarchical authority and more on participative methods, they have the right to expect the same change to occur in their relationship with their seniors.

A final problem is how to ensure a fair balance of representation in any participative body. There is the practical problem of having a body small enough to be effective and yet large enough to accommodate the different interest groups. More generally, there is the difficulty of identifying these separate interest groups and of allowing for the fact that they will change. The traditional divisions on pay and conditions such as men/women, worker/management, skilled/semi-skilled, day/shift, clerical/manual, production/trades, and so on are grounded in industrial history, but many issues cut across them and the people in these categories will align themselves in different ways according to the subject discussed.

A good example of the failure of traditional groupings to give an important category of people a voice has been the immigrant workers in Europe. Although there are about 8 million immigrant workers in Europe with 4 million dependants, they cannot make themselves felt through the established systems of representation on the issues that particularly concern them. This led in 1973 to their forming separate organisations and taking industrial action in France and Germany.[14] There is no simple answer to ensuring a fair balance of representation in a participative structure, but the essential point is that there should be some mechanism to allow the balance to change in response to changes within the working community. Thus, participation in management must offer genuine and equal opportunities to everyone in a given industrial community to involve themselves in the working of the participative system. Different degrees of participation offend against the concept of participation itself. The principle is simple and self-evident, but it can only be seen working in a small number of unusual enterprises like the

69

Scott-Bader Commonwealth.

This is an appropriate place at which to comment on the role of the law in promoting participative management. A legal obligation to set up works councils in firms of a certain size or to appoint employee representatives to the boards of public companies would establish formal procedures, but would not guarantee that life would be breathed into them. Its main advantage would lie in the firm declaration of public policy it would represent; its disadvantages are that it would focus attention on the provision of institutions rather than on their work and that it would tend to standardise forms of participation and inhibit experimentation. Here I support the practical view, expressed in the TUC interim report, on the argument for a mandatory system of employee representation —

'At the same time it must be recognised that each industry
has its own unique features and any system has to be
flexible enough to take account of these differing realities.'

Effective participation depends on the attitude of the participants' approach. This is outside the scope of the law; but an indirect way in which the law can raise management standards is by backing practical principles of conduct, as it has done with the Code of Industrial Relations Practice.

Decision-Making and Participation

So far the discussion has concentrated on the mechanics of the participative system. It is equally important to consider how the system will work when set up: in which decisions do people want to participate, who wishes to participate in them, how will they be trained to do so and what information will they need? We can then conclude with what the effects on business organisations are likely to be.

The priorities for participation cannot be settled in advance, because they must be determined by the participants. Participation is progressive both in the issues with which it deals and its growth within the enterprise. This is why I favour its introduction at shop-floor level. At the works level the advantages of participation in the

70

management of such activities as safety and training are equally clear-cut. Once participation has cut its teeth in these initially unexciting fields, it can broaden its scope and lengthen its time-scale to review the performance of the unit concerned and its future prospects. If participation starts with abstract issues like long-term plans, there will be no visible results to establish confidence. The fundamental point about priorities is that they will change and the participative system must respond to such changes. Nevertheless, there is a distinction between types of decision; the executive decision and the policy decision. The daily sales and production decisions are examples of executive decisions. In arriving at them, the objective is to define the limits as narrowly as possible. This allows decision-taking to be delegated and to be more speedy, by excluding any issues not directly relevant to solving the immediate problem. This order of decision is well suited to participative management, as the decisions are in areas of importance to the employees concerned, and they are grounded in fact. I see progress being mainly made in relation to executive decisions through the increased downward delegation of these decisions, so encouraging participation in them. For this to be successful the flow of information will have to be improved and redirected. Participation will not however rest there: it may be easy to agree on the best way of meeting a given order in a given time, but if participation is encouraged it will question its limits — was this the right order to have taken in the first place? Such a question not only transfers the participative level upwards, but it undermines the basis of the system for taking executive decisions by extending its boundaries.

With policy decisions, such as defining the aims of the company and how they are to be achieved, the problem is different. It becomes one of ensuring that participation takes place early enough in the decision-making process for it to be effective. Reading some of the literature on participation, I was struck by the lack of analysis of how policy decisions are made in practice. The impression given is that policy decisions are simply high level executive decisions, which might be taken at a board meeting after circulating a paper

71

summarising the facts, figures and arguments. If this were so, attendance at such meetings would provide all that was required for full participation. Policy decisions are however quite different from executive decisions. The object is to allow those involved in arriving at them to range unrestricted over as many outcomes as possible. This in turn means that policy decisions are not reached at a single, formal meeting, but evolve over a period through a number of specific and chance discussions. The time-scale of policy decisions and the way in which they are arrived at make them difficult to fit into a participative system, yet they are an essential aspect of participation, because once taken they set the limits for executive decisions.

The experience of encouraging participation in town planning is interesting in this context. It illustrates the issues that will arise, if less acutely, with participation in industrial management. For example, in preparing its Structure Plan, Birmingham took the unusual step of attempting to obtain ordinary people's views on the shape that the City should take. The City Council drew up a statement of objectives in population, housing, industry and employment and provided a summary of the key, background facts. They then posed a number of questions on specific priorities which led up to a choice of planning options, both short- and long-term. As far as I know this is the first attempt on any scale to take a consumer approach to civic planning and it forms an admirable precedent. The process did however bring out how difficult it is to reduce complex issues, where the variables interact and which have a long time-scale, to a form suitable for making a single choice or for ranking by preference. In effect, policy decisions cannot be reduced to executive decisions, without eliminating many of the possible solutions, including perhaps just that solution which the exercise of participation was designed to elicit. The questionnaire and choice of options also showed that in longer-term planning, participation at a point in time and applied to a few major decisions is of limited effectiveness. The decisions themselves are to a great extent determined by earlier decisions. More fundamentally, planning is a continuous process and so participation in it must also be continuous if it is to influence that forming of opinions and the elimination of alternatives which characterise policy decisions. Also in the Birmingham planning experience only 3,600 completed questionnaires were received from the public, when more than 1,000,000 people live in the city.

At this point, I would like to refer to an important comment on participative planning and decision-making made by Mr. Eli Goldston, the founder of these lectures, in a talk on 'America's Energy Crisis and Europe'.[15] He underlined the need for a more rational approach to resolving the conflict between the environment and the demand for energy and summarised the problem as follows:

'Our decisional apparatus is set up to decide whether the oil refinery or the liquefied natural gas storage or some other form of 'skunk works' would be built at 'A'. Everybody opposed to putting it at 'A' comes in to participate and it is decided not to build it at 'A'. The process is repeated for 'B' and it is decided not to build it at 'B'. Similarly it is decided not to build it at 'C' or 'D' and all the way to 'Z'. What we are now in the process of developing is a decisional apparatus that will consider the possibilities from 'A' to 'Z' in one proceeding, weigh the relative cost and benefits at each location, and ultimately settle on 'F' or 'U' or 'Y' as not the desirable place to build it but as the least undesirable place to build it and where society therefore requires that it be built'.

This summary brings out two essential points. First, participation is not simply a euphemism for forming a pressure group; in fact pressure-group tactics are normally opposed to genuine participation since they are used by a single-minded minority to establish its point of view, whether or not the less well-organised majority agrees. The pressure group is not concerned with the essentially two-way nature of participation. Its collective mind is made up and it has no wish to listen to other opinions or interests. Second, participation involves taking responsibility for reaching a decision, as Mr. Goldston so clearly brings out. Representing a point of view is not participation

73

and participative management requires decisions to be made, even if the consequences will not be in the immediate interests of a particular group of those participating, as with the siting of the 'skunk works'.

The Extension of Participation

The small response that Birmingham received to its experiment in participative planning raises the question of how many people wish to participate in management and whether the pressure for participation is as real as I have assumed? I do not suggest that the arguments for participation depend on numbers, but the proportion of employees who will participate actively is relevant. On the evidence available, there seems to have been a ready response to opportunities for participation at the shop-floor level and this should extend participation further back into the decision-making process and over a broader range of issues. As the level rises, more must be interested in direct participation in their own work situation, while the number who are prepared to participate in a representative capacity will be more limited. Nevertheless, experience of direct participation will increase those prepared to participate as representatives. Only certain people will come forward to represent their fellows and they will be motivated by the wish to represent rather than the origin of the representations. There need be no conflict between increased participation and established arrangements for collective bargaining, since many of the same people will carry out both functions.

Those who by nature have an interest in participation will be attracted to places of work where they can exercise it and those who prefer a more regulated existence will move out. The distribution of people among companies may be more influenced by reaction to their way of life than is generally thought. It would be interesting to study an institution like Glacier Metals, to weigh up how far a particular approach to work and its organisation is reinforced through the self-selection of its employees. It would also be reasonable to expect

74

participation to vary with the state of the company and for a threat to security to lead to a higher degree of involvement, because an abstract issue — the future shape of the business — had become an immediate and concrete one. The attitude to collective participation, however, is likely to differ basically between those who see themselves as having a long-term stake in their present place of employment and those who are in no way tied to their current job. These expectations may or may not be fulfilled, but they must affect the relationship that an individual sees himself as having with his company and help to determine his time horizon over participation.

Views on the value of length of service have changed interestingly in the last fifty years. In the 1920s and 1930s, when there was every incentive for employees to remain with their companies, length of service was important in pay and conditions. It has diminished in the last twenty years, although companies now have incentives to encourage it. Given a greater degree of participation length of service may again become more highly valued, because employees (and potential pensioners) will be critically interested in its future and because their experience and knowledge will enable them to participate more effectively than those with shorter service. Also, participation will be built on the growth of trust and confidence between individuals and if there are advantages in continuity among employee representatives, there are equal advantages in continuity among the managers with whom they work. Clearly a variety of experience is an important feature of management development, but I would expect managers and career planners in participative companies to give increasing weight to the dislocation of relationships caused by frequent management moves.

Training for Participation

Discussion of who is to participate must lead to the key issue of training. Participation in management will require board backing and careful planning, but above all it will depend on training, to give the best possible chance of making a success of the participative approach. The training needs of managers under a participative system are clear enough and have been touched on in discussing the reactions of managers to its introduction. They will operate within a structure of authority which is less well-defined, but which offers the chance to win a higher degree of commitment from the working group. Managers will have to rethink their approach to setting goals, providing leadership and solving problems in the light of a new framework of expectations. Some will not be able to meet the demands of an enabling rather than a directing role, or will lack the conviction to try to do so. The major elements in their training programme will be principles of participation and the lessons from applying it. Training must also be available to representatives and individuals who want to improve their ability to participate in the company's affairs. They will need to learn more about its operations and about the political and business constraints within which it must be run. Any study of a business that successfully uses participative methods, like the John Lewis Partnership, brings out the importance of a free flow of information in both directions and of the right to question. Information, however, is of limited use without some help in how to interpret it. One cannot question effectively without knowing what to ask.

I attach particular importance to training for participation for two reasons. First, because participation demands more of the individual manager than the traditional form of management. Training is needed to achieve the required change in approach and to provide the manager with the necessary skills. Participation in management will succeed only where training has been thorough. Failure will, no doubt, be blamed on the participative approach and not to inadequate planning and preparation. Second, participation offers an opportunity to combine the aims of individuals and those of their enterprise; this contrasts with the normal process of collective bargaining. Participation is therefore a unifying influence within the business. There is no reason why the training of everyone affected by the introduction of participation should not be carried out jointly. It is illogical for the training of managers and of union officials or employee representatives to be separate, so reinforcing differences of background and outlook, particularly at more senior levels. The quality of the training would be improved by drawing on a wider range of experience, where the nature of managers' and officials' jobs tends to converge.

The failure to achieve this even at senior levels may be due to the belief that it would be a form of indoctrination, designed to break down differences of view that ought to be maintained. If this is the reason, it is based on a misunderstanding about the nature of training, since training will clarify differences in responsibility between managers and representatives and so sharpen rather than blur them. It would achieve a better understanding of the background against which both groups have to carry out their tasks and a mutual appreciation of each other's methods of thinking and approach. When conflicts do arise, there is then more chance of their being about the real issues and of being kept within the bounds of what is negotiable. Training for participative management cannot raise even illusory fears of indoctrination, so there is no reason why it should be segregated. A common training experience would help to develop the personal relationships on which participation must be based.

Implications of Extending Participation

What is the effect of the introduction of participation in the management of an enterprise on its development? Ralf Dahrendorf said in a recent lecture:

'Indeed I suspect that total participation may well mean total immobility for any social unit.'[16]

In a business context I would certainly expect increased participation eventually to alter a company's nature. Participation, following Ralf Dahrendorf, will exercise a conservative rather than an innovative influence over an enterprise's development. It is likely to favour growth at home rather than growth overseas and organic growth rather than growth by acquisition. Participation would affect particularly the question of size; it would put a brake on major

77

mergers and would not accept the logic of increasing the size
of companies and their units as self-evident. This attitude reflects the
search for security in an economic environment, which appears to
be increasingly dominated by large international companies. Quite
apart from distrusting size, especially on an international scale
because it is associated with a lack of security and a low degree of
response, two practical aspects of participation tend to reinforce
this attitude. First, it is easier to build up the personal relationships
and informal contacts favourable to participation in a smaller rather
than a larger unit. Second, the mechanics of representative
participation become much harder the moment a unit adds a new
layer of representation. The lines of communication become longer and
it is that much more difficult to reconcile the number of interest
groups with a unit council of workable size.

Increased participation may do no more than make British
industry more responsive to views which are becoming widely
held in the community as a whole, about economic growth,
the balance between overseas development and the size of companies.
The key point is that companies advocating an increased degree of
participation in management should think through its likely longer-
term consequences on their own development. Many attempts to
introduce participation will come to nothing because of the inherent
difficulties of this approach to management. They will represent
the failure of good intentions to be adequately backed by commitment
and training. To introduce participation into an enterprise, however,
while being out of sympathy with the kind of policies that the
participants will press for, would be peculiarly short-sighted. The
effects of increased participation in management on the structure
and objectives of British business is just one field of study related to
participation where the analytical and research abilities of the
academic world would be welcome. This lecture has left many loose
ends which would usefully be followed up. There would be clear
advantages if the research into participation and the monitoring of
it in practice were to be co-ordinated by a joint management-trade
union body sponsored by the CBI and the TUC on the Norwegian
model.

78

I believe that participation in management is not a passing phase. From the standpoint of the individual, who is deeply concerned about the meaning of work and the place of industry in society, participation offers the opportunity to become involved and to take responsibility for the way in which industry should develop. From the company's point of view participation can harness forces which at present are hardly tapped; in J.W. Humble's words 'The most underutilised resource in business is the ability people have to improve themselves and their jobs in an imaginative and creative way.'

Finally, at a time when we must be more than ever conscious of the negative powers that both employees and employers possess, participation can restore a sense of common purpose and provide the unifying influence that business needs if it is to meet the continually rising expectations of the community. The greatest mistake we could make is to underestimate the difficulties of introducing participative management into British industry. The concept is simple, the mechanics of putting it into practice are complex and contentious. Participation in management will progress only if the commitment to it is wholehearted and sincere and if the training effort is in proprotion to the magnitude of the task. The debate about participation in management is important, not only because the approach has so much to offer to individuals, to their representative organisations and to companies, but also because it will markedly influence the future development of British business.

NOTES

1. *The European Approach to Worker-Management Relationships*, British-North American Committee, 1973.
2. Sir Leonard Neal referred to the MP who asserted that the establishment of statutory Works Councils would release 'a tidal wave of enthusiasm for work at the shop floor level'.
3. 'What managers think of participative leadership', Larry E. Greiner, *Harvard Business Review*, March/April, 1973.
4. *Participation & Manpower Policy*, OECD, 1969.
5. Rt. Hon. Reg. Prentice: *Participation and British Industry*, Financial Times Conference, 1973.

6. For example, the advantage of smaller-sized units and the disadvantage of business objectives that are less capable of being influenced by the average employee.
7. Works Councils, Employee Directors, Supervisory Boards, IPA, 1973.
8. F. Chaney and K. Teel, 'Participative Management – A practical experience', *Personnel,* November/December, 1972.
9. Ibid.
10. *Industrial Democracy,* Interim Report by the TUC General Council, 1973.
11. In the same way the constitution of the Bournville Works Council is prefaced by: 'The first duty of the Works Council, Divisional Consultative Committees and Departmental Committees shall be to encourage and establish good relations and mutual trust between non-Management and Management and to foster and maintain a spirit of cooperation, thus promoting the welfare and prosperity of the Bournville community'.
12. TUC Evidence to Donovan Commission, 1966.
13. The 1973 strike at the Hoogovens Steelworks in Holland by 1,500 key workers was in support of a claim for all pay increases throughout the organisation to be redistributed so that everyone would receive a uniform cash payment: the stated aim of the strike was 'to force a fundamental change in the Dutch political and economic system and eventually to make the concept of social equality a practical reality'.
14. These immigrants are mainly young and are willing to do jobs that have become difficult to staff with nationals. Their hosts need their labour but do not wish them to settle with the consequential costs of education and pensions, so they have the dilemma of recognising the scandalous conditions in which many of the immigrants live, but fearing that improvements in these conditions will encourage further immigration.
15. Given in London on 31 May 1973.
16. 'Organisation, change and democracy: the experience of the European Communities', 1973 Joan Woodward Memorial Lecture.

80

APPENDIX

Participation in Cadbury Schweppes

It may be helpful to add a postscript outlining briefly the structure
for participation in the home operations of Cadbury Schweppes.
It is based on works or joint councils at the various units which make
up the company and it supplements well-established arrangements for
collective bargaining. The aim is to have a forum at each level in the
home company for a representative cross-section of all the employees
on a given site or in a particular product grouping to meet regularly
with those with a direct responsibility for the running of their
operation. The councils are elected and represent the main interest
groups within the home business.

Cadbury Schweppes employs about 30,000 people in the
United Kingdom. The business is divided by product into four main
operating Groups – Confectionery, Drinks, Tea & Food, Health
& Chemical – with some smaller separate divisions and company
central services including the head office of the Overseas Group,
which coordinates the company's activities outside the UK. The
participative structure follows the organisational pattern of the
company, but it is not uniform throughout the business. Although
the company has a common purpose in respect of participation,
the mechanics of implementing it vary according to the history and
background of the units.

Shop-floor participation in matters directly connected with the
work of an individual department is organised more or less formally
in each of the factories: at Bournville, for example, because of its
size, departments have their own departmental committees, which
head up to divisional consultative committees and so to the Works
Council itself.

Chart 1 shows diagramatically how the participative system is
structured from the plant or factory level upwards and gives an idea

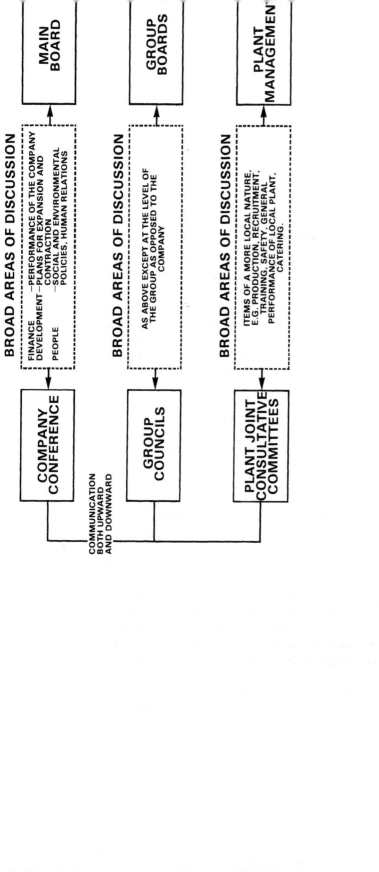

MAIN BOARD

BROAD AREAS OF DISCUSSION

FINANCE —PERFORMANCE OF THE COMPANY
DEVELOPMENT—PLANS FOR EXPANSION AND
CONTRACTION
PEOPLE —SOCIAL AND ENVIRONMENTAL
POLICIES, HUMAN RELATIONS

COMPANY CONFERENCE

COMMUNICATION
BOTH UPWARD
AND DOWNWARD

GROUP BOARDS

BROAD AREAS OF DISCUSSION

AS ABOVE EXCEPT AT THE LEVEL OF
THE GROUP AS OPPOSED TO THE
COMPANY

GROUP COUNCILS

PLANT MANAGEMENT

BROAD AREAS OF DISCUSSION

ITEMS OF A MORE LOCAL NATURE,
E.G. PRODUCTION, RECRUITMENT,
TRAINING, SAFETY, GENERAL
PERFORMANCE OF LOCAL PLANT,
CATERING.

PLANT JOINT CONSULTATIVE COMMITTEES

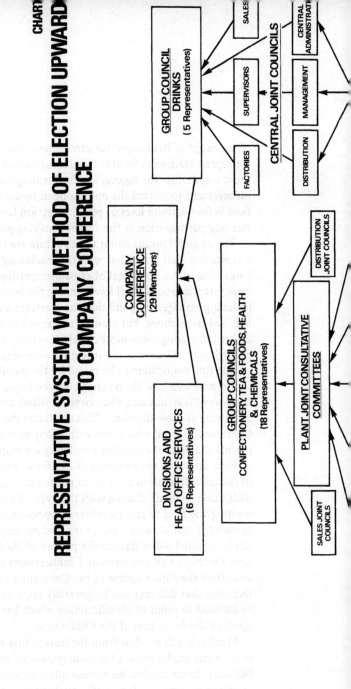

of the range of items open for discussion at each level. The object is for representatives to be able to raise matters of concern to them with those responsible for making the final managerial decisions and for the management to discuss the options open to them in any particular field before definite lines of policy or action have been formed. In this way participation in the decision-making process can take place.

The essential points about the structure are that it is two-way, that it is elective, that it coexists with the machinery for collective bargaining with a good deal of cross-membership, that it represents the main interest groups at all levels among the home-based employees including management, and that the meetings are regular. It was not imposed from above, but grew on an experimental basis from discussion among those most closely involved in joint consultation throughout the business and it is still developing its role.

The first major item to be raised by the members of the Company Conference was how the balance between home and overseas investment is struck and what considerations are taken into account in arriving at these decisions. This illustrates the ability of the Conference to deal with issues with a long time horizon, for which the normal channels of collective bargaining are inappropriate. It is also an issue on which the members of Conference required a good deal of factual information in order to participate on more equal terms with those regularly dealing with this type of problem and a specific meeting was held to give members an opportunity to do so. The knowledge that we now have a forum where major Company decisions can be debated will influence the pattern of those decisions. I am clear therefore that the views and deliberations of the Conference will affect the future course of the Company's development, but I recognise that this may not be generally apparent, since it will always be difficult to point to specific action which has been taken as a result of the formation of the Conference.

Finally, it will be clear from the lecture that I do not believe that there is one model system for participation of universal application. Not only do we need to learn from different approaches to the provision of a greater degree of participation, but it must also be right for companies to develop their own institutions on the basis of whatever consultative or negotiating machinery they already have. Cadbury Schweppes was in a position to built on a joint consultative structure of long standing, which had established its role over time, which had worked in harmony with the trade unions and which had earned the confidence of its constituents. I can see all the difficulties that stand in the way of introducing a similar structure if the same roots are not there; nevertheless it is open to any company to develop its management and operating systems in the direction of encouraging a greater degree of participation.

4. TRADE UNIONISM AND THE MULTINATIONAL COMPANY

J.L. Whitty

Introduction

In spring 1971 there was a strike at Ford's of Dagenham. It was a strike not without significance for the national economy, for it represented a major challenge to the Conservative administration's 'informal incomes policy'. Up until that point the policy had been largely successful in reducing the level of wage settlement in the public sector and Fords was regarded by many commentators as being a crunch case in the private sector. But in the long run, it was a strike which many have seen as being of more significance in an international context. In 1969 the management of British Ford had attempted to introduce, through the courts, a legally binding contract on their workers. This attempt had failed. At the time, the influence of the management of American Ford in the tactics of the local management had been discerned by most commentators. Since then, however, Ford of Britain had repeatedly asserted their independence from the international management in Dearbourne in personnel management.

In 1970, in a significant — if indirect — indication of the strength of multinational organisation, the company was able to defeat a strike in their UK supplier by importing the component — a large die-cast from Germany — at short notice.[1] The 1971 dispute made it clear that, despite the proclaimed autonomy of the personnel managers in Ford of Britain, the attitude of the international management of Ford to the personnel problem at their British plants was a key factor. This was dramatically emphasised when Henry Ford II himself arrived in the UK. Perhaps most symbolic of all was the treatment he received from the British Government. Ford was given facilities normally considered appropriate for a visiting Head of State. He visited the Prime Minister at 10 Downing Street to discuss the dispute. In his public utterances, however, he scarcely

86

repaid this hospitality with the kind of tactful diplomacy normally expected of visiting dignitaries. He stated, 'there is nothing wrong with Ford of Britain — only with the country . . . we can't recommend any new capital investment in a country constantly dogged with labour problems.' He threatened to switch investment out of the UK, sometimes claiming the alternative location would be Europe, sometimes South-East Asia, or South America. By threatening to use the management flexibility of the multinational to divert production and new investment away from Britain, Henry Frod was explicitly escalating the local conflict within British Ford onto a new international plane.

Within days, the dispute was also escalated on the trade union side. Quite fortuitously, it happened that the Automotive Section of the International Metal-workers Federation was meeting at TUC Headquarters in London. Present were trade union representatives of France, Germany, Belgium and the United States. Leonard Woodcock, General Secretary of the United Automobile Workers of America, was a key figure at that meeting. During the course of the meeting, German and Belgian unions expressed their solidarity with their British counterparts by refusing to accept any switch to production from the UK during the course of the strike. The United Automobile Workers supplemented this by offering pressure and support from the United States. If the strike should continue, financial support was also promised. The outcome of this was that Leonard Woodcock was likewise invited to No. 10 to discuss the problems. By receiving first Henry Ford II then Leonard Woodcock, the British Government, for the first time, recognised the new dimension that the growth of multinational companies have brought to British industrial relations.

On one level all these comings and goings were a charade. In the event, the strike was ultimately settled in the normal way — by negotiation between a British company and British trade unions. The result was not as much as the workers claimed, but significantly more than the Government had hoped to see this pace-setting settlement concede. The following year, incidentally, was one of the most profitable ever for Ford in Britain.

87

On another level, however, the extension of the 'bluff and counter-bluff' of industrial relations to an international plane was of profound significance. It symbolised a new triangle of forces which could increasingly come to bear on large sectors of many manufacturing industries: the highly-organised and flexible management of multinational companies able to divert and re-source production, and to integrate production in many countries within a single global plan; the spontaneous and largely unorganised, nevertheless potentially powerful use of international trade union cooperation, and the enforced acquiescence of the nation-state in the plans of the multinational and in the collective bargain that was ultimately reached. The dramatic nature and explicitness of this global escalation is almost unique to Fords. But as a new dimension to labour relations, it may not be so for much longer.

This paper attempts to analyse this new dimension.

The Growth of the Multinationals

'Multinational' commercial, trading and financial enterprises are older than capitalism itself. But the phenomenon of multinational location of manufacturing capacity is of relatively recent origin. Their growth represents both the internationalisation and the concentration of capital. Prior to the Second World War, what we now call multinational companies were rare and in relatively specialised sectors such as electrical engineering where the tentacles of General Electric were spread all over the world. The main pattern of pre-war internationalisation of capital (even with General Electric) was through portfolio investments. The main forms of concentration of capital on the other hand were the creation of large nationally-based firms. And the main form of control that these firms had over international trade was effected through the systematic creation of cartels.

Since 1945, some of these features have remained. But a new pattern has predominated. The emphasis in overseas investments by all capital-exporting countries has been on *direct* rather than portfolio investment; control and distortion of international trade has been through the internal transactions of the new multinationals, rather than by a formation of cartels. Concentration of capital into strong *nationally*-based companies has, of course, continued — increasingly abetted by interventionist governments and the growing importance of public sector contracts — but concentration into multinational grouping has nevertheless outstripped this movement.

In one respect it is strange that multinational companies have flourished in an era of historically low and diminishing tariff barriers such as we have seen since the war. But although the motive of 'jumping the tariff wall' by investing overseas might be reduced, other imperatives have been much stronger: the need to maximise product life by offsetting technological obsolescence by ever-widening of the market; the need to have a rapid access to large markets to maximise benefits of new production technology; in accelerating search for the minimum costs, labour, finance, and materials to meet the increasing domestic competitiveness that low tariffs and expanding world trade imply. For all these reasons, the post-war period has increasingly been the era of multinational.

Inevitably, any discussion of multinationals tends to concentrate on American-owned multinationals. This contribution is no exception, since 70 per cent of major multinationals are US-owned, and many of the industrial relations problems have arisen with US-owned multinationals. Nevertheless, it should be remembered that British-owned multinationals form the second largest group, and there are increasing numbers of West European — and more recently Japanese — companies. Each multinational has its own style and its own managerial philosophy, which often reflects its national origin and its early history, however truly multinational its present production pattern may be. In some of the generalisations that follow, these differing origins and different management ideologies should be borne in mind.

The behavioural characteristics of multinationals — or some multinationals at least — also present a marked change in the assumptions of economists. Charles Levinson, General Secretary of the International Chemical Workers whose activities have done much to increase an awareness of the problems presented by

89

multinationals, has identified the clear tendency — perhaps most marked in the process industries with which he is concerned — for multinationals' main objective to be concerned not so much with maximisation of profit, but the maximisation of corporate growth and cash flow.[2]

Two very importance consequences arise from these changes. Firstly, there is an increasing tendency for multinational groupings which initially were often combined by ownership alone to be transformed into ever more centralised single managerial entities. The rate at which this occurs, and the efficiency with which it occurs, differ very widely between different multinational companies, but as an overall tendency, it is unmistakable; there is now in most leading multinational companies a global corporate plan. Secondly, the relationship between a multinational company and the nation-state is entirely different from that of a nationally-based firm (albeit organised in a cartel) and the nation-state. In the latter instance, the interest of the parent country and the enterprise will often coincide. With the multinational company, the divergence of interests can be acute. In an era of multinational enterprise, it is difficult for even the most ardent defender of free enterprise to claim that 'what is good for General Motors is good for America' or for any of the other 106 nations in which General Motors are located.

The Impact of Multinationals on the Work-Force

It is important to recognise that for a company which seeks to reach or protect a world market, the 'typical' multinational response of multiple location of production is by no means the only option open. There is a range of responses including large-scale licensing, contracting to factoring firms, agency arrangements and, of course, the option of a cartel or partial cartel. All large multinationals adopt a mixture of these approaches at different times and in different markets. This contribution, however, is concerned with the effect on the work-force, and the response of the trade union movement to only one of these options, the one which defines the typical multinational, i.e. the location of production capacity in different national economies, and the organisation of these various locations into a single managerial unit, however

90

loosely integrated.

Because of the organisation of multinationals into single management entities, and because of this change of relationship between such enterprises and the national economy, it is reasonable to assume that workers collectively and trade unions as institutions would be forced to adapt their attitudes because of the growth of multinationals. Theoretically one can immediately identify a number of issues and tensions that this process would create for trade unions.

First, there is the tendency for a multinational management to attempt to impose personnel and collective bargaining practices on overseas subsidiaries which are alien and contrary to the practice in the host countries. In particular, the attitude of a certain American-owned multinational towards trade union recognition very much reflects the American experience, and the success of certain highly profitable companies in maintaining a degree of anti-union paternalism is almost unknown in large companies in Western Europe.

Second, the more rapid transfer of technological advance and the standardisation of organisational behaviour following the spread of multinationals can cause problems of adjustment, particularly when they are imposed by new management. Third, and perhaps more significantly, there is the change in the balance of power between management and labour. This is perhaps just the latest stage in a process whereby first labour and then management have both increased and decreased the area of conflict to their own advantage – from the individual to the work-group to the plant, from the plant to the company and – where it suited one side or another – back again. The ability to translate local conflicts on to an international frame, by threats to switch short-term production or long-term investment, represent a major shift in the flexibility of bargaining which has accrued almost entirely to the management side.

Fourth, there is the strain that the imposition of a multinational dimension places on relations betweens the work-force employed by multinationals and those employed by local enterprise. This is a strain particularly in many of the developing countries. Fifth, there is the much more fundamental long-term problem of how the increasing concentration of investment decisions in the hands of fewer

and fewer multinational companies, planning their resources on a
global basis, will affect the international specialisation of labour, and
the international specialisation of production and trade. The advent
of the multinational has substantially modified the whole pattern
of international trade. The effects of multinationals' decision-taking
seriously upsets the more simple theories of comparative advantage,
as the basic unit of production in trade terms ceases to be the
nation-state, and becomes instead a multinational corporation. This
undermines conceptions about the balance of labour skills in a
world context, and in turn has made obsolete many of the
trade policies of GATT that are based on these theories.

Last, there are the political implications. In Western Europe, at least,
the trade unions have been to the forefront in calling for a greater
degree of state intervention and centralised planning of the economy.
The ability of the nation-state to conduct such a planning exercise,
and to take the necessary measures and be prepared to use the
necessary sanctions to ensure that it is fulfilled has been severely
constrained by the growth of multinationals. The ability to use
centralised planning, state ownership and state intervention as
means of furthering socialist priorities, to which most West
European trade unions are committed, is thus also severly constrained.
It is important to recognise that a trade response to multinationals
is not just a response to their labour relations and personnel
procedures. It is a response to the total fact of the multinationals'
existence.

The theoretical implications of multinationals for the world
labour force just described sounds cataclysmic. In practice, the
effects have been considerably less dramatic. It would be helpful
to look at the experience of three different regions and look at
the effects of multinational operations on the work-force and
collective bargaining in these three regions in detail — remembering
that trade union response tends to be on all issues at two levels:
the direct response, and their influence via the political institutions.
The three regions taken are the UK (as representative of Western
Europe), South-East Asia and the USA.

The *United Kingdom* as the most complex of Western European economies in its international ramifications, is also parent to a larger number of multinational companies than any other country, apart from the USA. In terms of overseas investments per head of the population, we have by far the largest stake in home-grown multinationals of any country (Switzerland included). In 1973 new outward direct private investments reached the astounding level of £1,139 million. But the UK is also the recipient of substantial inward investment, and approximately one-sixth of British manufacturing industry is in the hands of foreign-owned multinationals, particularly of course American-owned. *South-East Asia* contains a number of countries which are almost totally dependent for their investment requirements on multinational investments. The *United States*, on the other hand, is obviously predominantly an exporter of capital and a parent country to multinationals. Inward investment, although growing rapidly, is relatively insignificant in terms of the total gross domestic capital formation within the USA and is still mainly in portfolio form.

The United Kingdom Experience

The attention of the TUC began to be drawn to multinational companies from 1968 onwards. In 1970 the TUC took the unusual step of calling a special conference on international companies. Papers presented and the contributions from the floor at that conference give some indications of the problems of industrial relations practices in certain foreign-owned companies in the UK.[3] An earlier TUC survey had shown that a substantial number of foreign-owned firms had refused trade union recognition and that they tended to be larger employers than the British firms where equivalent problems arose and tended to take a more systematic anti-trade union line than British firms in the equivalent position. A parent company's experience in the USA coupled with a high degree of paternalism in some cases such as IBM and Kodak were reflected in the behaviour of subsidiaries in the UK.

In one very important instance, that of Kodak, the TUC General Council have themselves become very much involved.

From 1967 onwards, representatives of the General Council attempted
to meet the management of Kodak. Kodak have effectively organised a
company union which, initially at least, was financed and sponsored
by the company. From time to time unions affiliated to the TUC
recruited substantial numbers of Kodak staff, when recruitment was
inhibited and hampered by the anti-union attitude of the company.
From 1972 onwards an attempt has been made to reach an
accommodation with the company, but this is as yet unsuccessful.
An even more blatant form of anti-union paternalism exists in UK
plants of other multinational companies, particularly IBM and the
international food and confectionery giant, Mars, whose secrecy
and anti-union propaganda to their own staff is quite extraordinary.

Although some large and significant companies such as these have
almost completely excluded trade unions, the most dramatic
difficulties have occurred with relatively small subsidiaries of small
multinationals. The most notorious episode between British
trade unionism and international companies have concerned
Roberts Arundel and Fine Tubes. In the first instance a twelve
month strike for recognition took place between 1967 and 1968,
but in January 1969 the parent company closed down the Stockport
Works and withdrew their capital to the United States. In the case
of Fine Tubes, the strike was even more prolonged, and it was
two years before any settlement was reached.

The TUC also cited in 1970 the following firms where
recognition problems have arisen: IBM, Gillette, Heinz, Fairchild,
Continental Oil, Goodyear, Firestone, Nestle and several
international airlines. In many of these instances, recognition was
concerned mainly with staff unions. Even now where recognition
problems exist, there have been on-going problems between the
management of a company such as Fords, which the local unions
tend to regard as reflecting the international nature of the company.
Ford have a history of resisting trade unions, and particularly
of resisting the power of shop stewards and work-place representatives.

For working people at the local level, the problem of international
companies is at its sharpest when existing British concerns are
acquired by foreign-owned companies. There is a real sense of

94

diminution of job security when it is known that decisions about jobs are taken much further away. There is also a tendency on the part of foreign managements to impose new working practices. When Chrysler carried out its takeover of Rootes in 1967, a strike broke out almost immediately in the Coventry works, due to a change in the piece-work to the then purely American wage practice of a measured day rate, without prior consultation of workers on the assembly line.

Of greater long-term significance is the alteration to the balance of power which for various reasons conflicts have shown occurring in the UK. The obvious form of this is the increasingly frequent threat to switch location of investment. Recent examples of this instance are the disputes at Massey-Ferguson in 1973 and at Chrysler (UK) in early 1974. On one level this is regarded now by unions and workers as the normal bluff in any dispute with multinationals. The short-term diversion of production or the threat to do so in response to a dispute is one thing, but the strategic direction of investment is another, and it is undoubtedly true that Britain has been receiving a declining share of the new investment on many US owned multinationals such as Fords and a number of UK and European-owned corporations (such as Plessey and Philips) and a share not reflecting the relative growth or profitability of the UK market. This investment has tended not to go to countries with so-called model industrial relations systems like Sweden or Germany, but to dictatorship countries like Spain and Brazil.

Industrial relations — and the allegedly poor record of UK labour — were part of the reason; how important a part only the corporate planners in the global corporation can say. But the changed balance of power reflects itself in other ways too. In addition to the industrial relations aspects, the British trade union movement has obviously been concerned about the effects on jobs. It is often claimed that the relatively foot-loose multinational companies have responded more flexibly to the incentive to regional investment in the UK than home-grown companies. This is in part true. One in eight jobs in Scotland is

95

now with an American-owned electronics company. However 'foot-loose' works both ways. The more mobile the industry the more likely it will eventually perceive advantages in moving still further afield. The problem with a number of multinational companies, American companies in Scotland in particular, is, as the TUC put it, that they have a rather cavalier attitude to redundancy. This has been the main drawback to relying on inward foreign investments to maintain the balance of payments. And it has had its effect on the industrial relations of the American-owned companies in Scotland which have *not* had a better record in industrial relations than the average; on the contrary, it appears that they have had a significantly worse record.[4]

There is also the longer-term impact of multinational investment on the kind of jobs that are available in the UK. A number of anxieties have been expressed that the North Sea Oil development, and in the past decade the electronics belt in Scotland was creating a form of 'coolie' labour drawn from Scotland, whereas some of the highly skilled management and technical jobs would be imported by the multinational companies, mainly from America.

But the most serious fear that the UK trade union movement has concerns not so much jobs directly as the lack of political control. Particularly in an era when we have a Labour Government, albeit a minority Labour Government, intending to extend the dimensions of government intervention through the 'planning agreements' system, and through the extension of direct public sector ownership in many sectors and companies via the National Enterprise Board, the apparent ability of multinational companies to escape, or at least substantially modify government control, must cause considerable anxiety. The TUC have always emphasised the need for close consultation on corporate planning with multinational companies and this is now being made explicit in the 'planning agreements' approach.

What of the effect of labour relations in the UK as a parent country to multinationals? Surprisingly, the main response to the multinational phenomen by the UK unions has been in relation

to inward investment by foreign-owned companies. In the USA much
of the American unions' attention has been directed at *'run-away
companies'* and it is surprising that British-owned multinational
companies with their high level of outward capital investment should
not have aroused more suspicion and antagonism amongst the trade
union movement. In 1971 and again in 1972, however, the TUC
adopted a resolution emanating from the Electrical Trades Union
to campaign against the danger of 'run-away companies' particularly in
the electronic and radio and television field.[5]

On the industrial relations front, there have been a number of
occasions when British trade unions have attempted to intervene,
with some success, in relation to the British-owned parent companies
abroad. Some years ago, intervention by the leading motor unions
with BMC averted a very nasty case of victimisation in BMC Chile
plant. More recently strenuous efforts have been made by trade
unions on behalf of workers in Hong Kong. This jewel of the British
colonial Empire still does not officially recognise trade unions.
The TUC in 1974 adopted a resolution calling for the application
of ILO conventions on organisational trade union rights
in Hong Kong.[5]

A further dimension to this is, of course, the location of
British-owned multinational companies in countries whose régime
can only be regarded as a dictatorship, or in the monority rule
countries of Southern Africa. In the past ten years a considerable
amount of pressure coming largely from TUC level has been brought
to bear on British-owned multinational companies operating in
South Africa. However, on the whole, this has been of a
generalised approach than to individual multinationals. This is,
however, changing and a number of British-owned multinationals are
having to respond to their own British trade unionists, by attempting
to justify their policy. The appallingly low level of wages paid by
these companies was revealed by the *Guardian* and other newspapers
and subsequently by Parliamentary Committee investigation
to be substantially below the line of the minimum levels
('Poverty Datum Line') set even by the South African government.[6]

The Impact on Developing Countries: South-East Asia

Until relatively recently the main impact of multinational companies on the developing world was at the raw material stage. Clearly the dominating feature of many developing economies was the predominance of one or more Western-owned companies in exploiting its own resources. The obvious examples are the oil companies in the Gulf, Nigeria and Venezuela; the United Fruit Company, of even older origin, in Guatemala and other central American republics; RTZ in Bougainville, the copper companies in Chile and Zambia and so on. More recently – almost entirely in the last five years in fact – we have had the phenomenon of the multinational manufacturing company moving into the Third World in a big way. The latest resting place of the 'run-away company' is South-East Asia. Taiwan has become dominated by American electronic companies, General Electric Company, General Instruments, RCA and so on. The Philippines, South Korea, Singapore – more with European-owned companies in the latter case such as Plessey and Phillips – have similarly been almost taken over by the electronic companies.[7]

On the surface the investment introduces a degree of affluence which otherwise might not have been attained by these countries. In fact in the perspective of history the migration of capital will almost certainly be seen to have had a disastrous effect on the industrialisation pattern and the labour relations pattern of these countries. They are almost entirely producing for the export market. They are products of a high level of technological achievement, but only transfer the lower value – added, high labour intensity part of that technology to the most developing country. They adopt the kind of production process which, far from raising the wages of local inhabitants as did the arrival of the oil companies or the extractive industries, appears to pay below even the going rate in these countries.[8] This is because of the relative labour intensity of the processes, and the relative reliance on female labour. This process is aggravated by the fact that the host governments, so anxious are they for investment, not only offer enormous capital grants, plus planning permission and tax concessions to the incoming multinationals, but also very frequently offer them 'concessions' on the labour relations. South Korea, Singapore and Indonesia are on occasions particular offenders in this respect. Even where there is an organised industrial relations system locally, multinationals are given a 'labour organisation holiday' for five years just as they are given 'tax holidays'. In South Korea and Indonesia there is no need for this. Independent trade union organisation has virtually been submerged in some of these countries and in virtually all of them its development is being inhibited. The well-intentioned liberal arguments directed against the AFL/CIO and against TUC unions expressing so-called protectionist policies in opposing 'run-away' companies need to be looked at very carefully. In many cases, the attraction to the company of the developing country to the multinational is a repressive regime and consequently quiescent work-force. Any preferential access Western countries give to the products that result from this arrangement serve to perpetuate it. Whether or not this is actually of benefit to peoples of the developing countries is a matter of political judgement.

What is clear is that neither this investment nor the trading concession necessarily benefits the developing countries to which it is directed. Moreover, the evidence tends to show that multinational companies in the developing world often represent an unhealthy political influence. As a blatant example, we have seen the activities of ITT and Kennicott in Chile.[9] Whatever the political judgement, it can also be seen that in some (though by no means all) developing economies their domination by multinational investment is in fact distorting, rather than enhancing, the development process by creating a distinctive sector of foreign investment, orientated almost entirely to Western consumer markets, and failing to integrate with or act as a stimulus to the rest of the economy.

United States Experience

At the other end of the process, the main concern of the American trade unions has been the effects of multinational company investments abroad on American jobs. The electronics industry, the radio and television industry and the textile industry have largely disappeared

99

from the United States. The initial move tended to be 'dual sourcing' in the Southern States and then in Mexico. The more favoured locations of American capital now appear to be South Korea, the Phillipines, Taiwan and to a lesser extent Singapore and Hong Kong. Indonesia is also building up its attractions in this sphere. The anxiety of the AFL/CIO at these developments has been labelled 'protectionist' in its crudest form. Its attitude is highly protectionist, but considerably more sophisticated expressions of anxiety and proposals for operational control of the multinationals have more recently been expressed both by the AFL/CIO and a number of its affiliates. The demands may sound merely protectionist, rejecting 'new preferential tariff agreements or the special arrangements that actually benefit multinational firms' but in reality the anxiety reflects a realisation that the multinational has introduced a new dimension into development economics.[10] Ironically, this happens at a time when the ALF/CIO itself is also beginning to become anxious about European investment in the USA.

The Trade Union Responses

At local level, trade union membership and organisation tends and will continue to tend to regard the multinational companies' local operations in much the same way it regards any other operation. There may on occasions be difficulties of recruitment due to virulent anti-union attitudes of certain multinational companies. However, in general terms, plant level negotiations with local management about issues which affect the plant alone can normally be conducted in the same way as they can with any domestic company. The problems arise once it becomes clear that the local management cannot, and in some cases will not, take the responsibility of making major decisions on industrial relations. This happens also with large multiplant firms within a single country, but the problem of communication is made much worse with multinationals. Hence we have local shop stewards and work-place representatives taking the initiative to contact their opposite numbers in the same multinational company but in other countries.

Sometimes this is done through the official trade union channel; sometimes quite *ad hoc;* sometimes through political contacts. Very firm links have been established between the Ford Shop Stewards Committee in the UK and workplace representatives and union officials in Germany, Belgium and France. Similar contacts at workplace level were established between the British and Italian unions with relation to the Dunlop/Pirelli merger.

It would be idle to pretend that such contacts and the ability to turn such contacts into any kind of successful action can flourish without the wholehearted backing and facilities of the official trade union movement. The very fact that such contracts are being established is of itself significant, but to give the trade unions sufficient muscle to be an efficient 'countervailing power', the organisation, apparatus and willpower have to be developed through the official control and internal structure of the movement. This section therefore attempts to examine how far the trade union movement internationally has responded both to the challenge of the multinationals and to the new perception of the challenge now manifest at grass-roots level.

The first point to recognise is that the trade union response to any change is on a number of different levels. The second is that, as already indicated, trade union attitudes towards multinationals are a response to the totality of their existence, not just to their direct impact on *collective bargaining.* The movement will, as in the past, attempt to organise *at the point at which decisions are really made,* and thus counter the global centralisation of multinational management. At the same time the movement is already organising itself to pressurise the international governmental agencies to try and restore a more stable balance between the interests of the nation-state and the multinational companies, operating in the *political* arena.

The Scope for International Trade Union Coordination

The trade union response will need to operate through the superstructure of the international trade union movement. The only alternative is for an entirely new superstructure to develop and at the

101

moment this appears unlikely. Before examining activity in this area, it is necessary to understand the relations between a number of complex institutions of the international movement.

In broad terms, we need to distinguish between International Confederations and International Trade Secretariats. An International Confederation is a confederation of national centres such as the TUC. There are three such international confederations each with its own ideological persuasion: ICFTU, WFTU and WCL; there is also the European Trade Union Congress covering Western Europe which contains elements of all three ideologies. In addition there are the International Trade Secretariats (with their WFTU equivalents, the Trade or Labour Internationals) which consist of affiliates who are *individual* trade unions organising in particular industries. It is this superstructure that is now being used to develop a more coherent trade union strategy towards the multinational. The ITS's — rightfully — receive the bulk of the publicity, and their activities have raised a perhaps somewhat premature terror amongst certain multinational companies.

It is certainly to the International Trade Secretariats that the trade union movement (and also most commentators) have looked for manifestations of the policy of countervailing power. Trade unions have always organised *at the place where decisions are made* and where the real power lies. Where management is internationalised it is suggested the strategy should thus be to internationalise collective bargaining. That at least is the simplistic argument. The machinery for doing this, for the ICFTU-affiliated unions, is clearly the International Trade Secretariat. These bodies until recently have been relatively shadowy. They are still small in terms of resources and support staff. But they represent an existing superstructure in the trade union movement through which a more coherent trade union strategy towards the multinational can be formulated. They are the mechanism whereby unions in a number of different countries can come together to react to the multinationals. Their original purpose was not this. They existed for the promotion of general international trade union understanding, and some exchange of experience at industrial level. Some would have said they were an unnecessary luxury. But with the advent of the multinational company the mechanism they provide is unique.

Many commentators insist on regarding the International Trade Secretariats as the counterpart of international companies. They are not. They are not even embryo international unions, though sometimes they are spoken of as such. They are not on the same plane as the international management of Ford or Dupont.

Power in the trade union movement rests, and will continue to rest, at the branch and in the individual factory; the General Secretary of the International Metalworkers can never be the equivalent of Henry Ford or Lord Stokes. There is no way whereby an equivalent managerial structure and organisational coherence can be imposed on the trade union movement at international level, in the way it is imposed by the company. To attempt to do so is to adopt a managerial-philosophy which is inappropriate to the reality of the trade union work. Nevertheless the ITSs represent a potential mechanism for the direction of power, for the acquisition and use of the information, and for the influencing of companies, governments and decision-makers in international politics. Countervailing power *is* being exerted, but in a different sort of power. To examine systematically activities at these levels it is useful to go back to the TUC Conference, in October 1970. At that Conference a number of different 'levels' of international coordination via International Trade Secretariats were evident. They were:

1. The collection of information.
2. The organisation of standing trade union 'World Councils' for multinationals.
3. *Ad hoc* international moves of solidarity if an affiliate was in dispute with a multinational (by financial aid, resisting switches of production, refusing additional overtime etc.).
4. Organisation of multinational consultative machinery.
5. International synchronisation of claims.
6. International harmonisation of non-wage collective bargaining objectives.
7. International co-ordination of industrial activities.

103

8. International harmonisation of wage objectives.
9. Presentation of internationally agreed bargaining demands and coordination of tactics to achieve these demands.

Of these, 1 and 2 were already well-established. There are examples of 3, 4 and even 6. The rest were largely hypothetical, although even by 1970 they were being discussed.

The TUC and the ICFTU at their World Conference in 1969 and 1971[11] also identified *political* objectives for the international movement which would be pursued largely by national centres and by the ILFTU. These included:

1. Observance of all International Labour Office Conventions by multinational companies.
2. Observance by multinationals of priorities of national social and economic planning.
3. Establishment of an ILO Study on the social and economic problems engendered by the growing powers of the multinational corporation.

These issues are discussed in the next Section:

The first area identified for action by ITSs by the TUC was the collection of *information*. The TUC stated then that almost all the International Trade Secretariats did collect and circulate information on multinationals. There is absolutely no doubt that their ability to do so and the quality of the information circulated four years later is substantially improved. The *International Metalworkers* (IMF) were always the leaders in this field as the largest international; they now provide a substantial amount of information not only on the structure of companies, having produced 20 to 30 detailed profiles on multinational companies in the engineering and electrical field, but also information on wage rates, and other conditions in different factories of the same multinational. The *International Food Workers* (IUF) jointly with the *International Chemical Workers* (ICF) service the World Council on Unilever and the information being brought together under its auspices provide an increasingly coherent picture of the vastly diversified operations of Unilever and their effect on the varying work-forces across the world. The ICF itself has now set up exchange of information for a large number of multinationals. The International Tailor and Garments Workers (ITGWF) in 1972 brought together massive information on three multinationals operating in their field: Courtaulds, BATA and C & A. The International white collar secretariat (FIET) also produce industry profiles on many of the multinationals within their area. This kind of information is extremely useful background, particularly useful to the small unions in developing countries, who are in countries where organisation and research is weak. There has also been a distinct improvement in the ability of the ITS to react to a developing situation, as a result of the improvement in the flow of information. It would now be true to say that the communication system and the ability to ask for *ad hoc* assistance within the International Metal Workers and the International Chemical Workers, for example, is now extremely good.

The organisation of *standing World Councils* on multinationals was the second area identified by the TUC. At that time the International Metal Workers were singled out as having gone the furthest in the creation of multinational 'World Councils'. This is still the case, though the ICF also have a large number of these bodies. Starting in 1966, the International Metal Workers established World Councils for the major American-owned automobile companies. This was followed by the Councils for the Japanese and European Companies. Although these bodies meet relatively infrequently, the information they generate is extremely useful, and by structuring the work they do, they are able to react to situations as they arise. This was instructive in the case of the meeting of the Joint World Councils in automobile industries in the case of Ford, cited at the beginning of this paper. *The International Petroleum and Chemical Workers* (IFPCW) (probably shortly to merge with ICF and the Food workers have all now set up World Councils in this area. One of the most recent is the establishment of the ICF World Council for Pilkington's in 1973. Pilkington's is very much a British-based company, but there was a recognition by the unions involved in Pilkington's (mainly the GMWU) that international ramifications were becoming an increasingly important background to negotiations within the UK.

The World Council was therefore set up in 1973, under the auspices of the ICF. The following lists the major World Councils or equivalent bodies known to have been set up by International Trade Secretariats and, where possible, the date of their institution.

International Trade Secretariats
World Councils and equivalent (for multinational companies)

International Metalworkers (IMF)		International Chemical Workers (ICF)	
Ford	(1966)	St. Gobain	(1967)
General Motors	(1966)	Michelin	(1969)
Chrysler	(1966)	Dunlop-Pirelli	(1971)
Volkswagen	(1966)	W.R. Grace	(1972)
Nissan-Toyota	(1968)	Rhone-Poulenc	(1972)
Fiat-Citroen	(1968)	Hoffnan-La Roche	(1972)
BMC	(1968)	Bayer	(1972)
Renault	(1968)	Michelin	(1972)
Volvo	(1968)	Du Pont	(1972)
General Electric	(1972)	Pilkington's	(1973)
Westinghouse	(1971)	Montedison	(1973)
Honeywell	(1971)	Shell	(1973)

Joint ICF/IUF	International Petroleum and Chemical Works (IPCW)	International Food Workers (IUF)	
Unilever (1972)	Shell	Nestlé	(1971)
	IBM		
(NB. In all, the ICF	Esso		
claim 15 World Councils	Dupont		
established and a	Union Carbide		
further 35 proposed.)			

The TUC then identified 'international solidarity moves'. In this category they referred to ad hoc moves whereby affiliates in dispute with international companies have received financial aid, negotiating help and made declarations of solidarity and taking action to resist switches of production and refusals to work additional overtime. There are an increasing number of examples in this area which have mainly been organised through the International Trade Secretariat. The *International Chemical Workers* have used pressure from their affiliates in the parent country to force concessions and union recognition in less well-organised areas, such as Turkey on multinational companies such as La Roche, Hoechst, Goodyear and even the highly paternalistic Michelin with their factory in Spain.[12] The *International Foodworkers* have had, over the years, a series of successive strikes: they forced recognition out of Inter-Continental Hotels (a Pan-Am subsidiary) in Liberia; the other way round, there was a case of a national strike in the USA against the National Biscuit Company (Nabisco) with messages of support from Nabisco plants in other countries, and actual coordination of strike action in Italy in the two Nabisco plants there — the pressure of Nabisco was sufficient to force them to settle in the USA. With the sacking of shop stewards by Pepsi-Cola in Uruguay, the pressure on Pepsi-Cola's parent company in America forced his reinstatement. More recently, the strike for union recognition in Texas against Farah International by the American Chemical Workers in 1973 was rendered successful by international pressure. Perhaps most significantly of all via the IUF and the ICFTU pressure was brought on Brooke Bond Liebig, to conduct *centralised* negotiations which they previously refused, so as to help unions in its massive plantations in Ceylon, where they paid very low wages.[13] *The International Metal Workers* have a run of similar small but significant successes. In most cases these involve trade union recognition or victimisation in areas where the union organisation was weak, whether in the metropolitan countries, like America, or more frequently in the new developing countries.

Although this records the successful actions, there have been a large number of unsuccessful ones. Particularly the failures relate to the inability to obtain reasonable trade union rights in dictatorship countries, like Spain, South Korea and Brazil.

The fourth area identified in 1970 was the development of *multinational consultations*. The model here was the discussion between the European Metalworkers Federation (which at that

107

time meant the ICFTU unions in the Common Market only) and the European management of Philips. Those negotiations were proceeding and had almost reached the point where they were effectively becoming negotiations about future company plans and about fringe benefits. However, predictably, at that point.they ran into a certain amount of trouble. On a consultative basis, the talks continue. However, the recent drastic cutbacks by Philips means all European operations (short-time working in most instances) did not occasion a meeting of this body, although it would seem that if this machinery were to develop this would be just the sort of situation that it would deal with. It must be admitted that hopes for this development have proved premature, and in any case, Philips was a very isolated example.

The more recent attempts to establish a similar dialogue with the European management of the Ford Motor Company have as yet met with no success. No formal bargaining was proposed but the management's attitude to the West European unions' suggestion of consultation was extremely hostile. The International Metalworkers claim 'that there was no doubt that the letter stating that the Ford Motor Company could see no advantage for it nor its employees in such a meeting was drafted in Detroit and not in the administrative offices of Ford Europe of Essex, England'. A more recent attempt in 1974 to establish such a dialogue also seems to have met with an entirely negative response by the Ford management. It cannot therefore be said that the internationalisation of the consultative process has developed very far in the last few years.

The TUC then referred to the possibility of *'synchronisation'* of collective agreements. With the pre-existing exception of United States/Canadian agreements, there has been only one rather minor example of such a development. Hailed by the ICF (quite accurately) as the first multinational agreement it concerns the Austrian-owned Rubber and Chemical Company, Semperit, where a joint agreement was reached between the company and unions in the Irish Republic and Austria. Another example already mentioned, is that of Brooke Bond Liebig, where some centralisation has occurred as far as developments on their plantations are concerned.

108

The TUC identified sixthly the coordination of *international industrial action*. The great example in this area is the now historic pattern of the French-owned (but Swiss-based) glass multinational of St. Gobain. It is worth repeating exactly what happened in this case. The French, German, Italian and American affiliates of the ICF agreed on a co-ordinated bargaining strategy towards the company.

The relevance of international union co-ordination of course depends on the way the multinational itself is organised. Broadly, there are two ways in which multinationals schedule their production. Either they have multiple sourcing and multiple plants making the same or similar products in different countries, or they have a partially or fully integrated systems where no single plant has the ability to produce a complete article. On the whole the trend amongst multinationals is from the former to the latter. This development greatly shifts the balance of power between the *state* (or purely domestic industry) and the multinational in favour of the multinational — which takes advantage of the cheapest and most efficient locations with respect to each particular part. But the effect on the potential balance of power between multinational and *organised labour* can be in the opposite direction. A strike of Fords in Britain can hold up production in Belgium and Germany now, whereas that was not true five years ago.

So far this ability to hit at a specialised area, with much more widespread, even global, repercussions has not been used to its fullest potential by the trade union movement. But with the development of international bilateral contacts between unions at local and national official level, it is almost certain that a more coherent approach to these potentialities will emerge. This is, of course, a short-term advantage. The multinational still has the flexibility to switch investment and production of the specialised part away from that particular location to another where the work-force is more quiescent. However, in many cases, the cost of so doing will be quite substantial, particularly when cash flow is such an important part of multinational operations. Whilst the long-term advantage remains with the multinational, the integration of production that now appears to be part of global planning process in a number of multinationals can rebound to the unions' favour. The successful development of international coordination of industrial action depends on the degree to which this can be exploited.

The final three categories of potential action set out by the TUC in 1970 have yet to become a reality. These were:

the harmonisation of non-wage collective bargaining objectives;
the harmonisation of wage objections;
the presentation of internationally agreed bargaining demands.

Only on the first could it be said that any progress was being made even on the trade union side. As the Philips experience has shown, companies are wary of moving from international 'consultations' to negotiations. Such a move also puts a strain on the solidarity unions where the more advanced countries might have to mark time whilst awaiting a levelling-up process, even within Western Europe. Within the IUF there is now some discussions on basic conditions for catering workers within the large hotel groups, such as Trust House Forte and Inter Continental, but they have not gone further than discussion.

The Present Positon

All of this means that the forecasts of certain commentators of the imminent advent of 'international collective bargaining' is somewhat premature. The chart opposite attempts to summarise the position, but this apparent lack of dramatic progress conceals the vastly increased resources and flexibility of International Trade Secretariats (or rather co-ordination between their affiliates since they still have few resources themselves). There will not be an 'International Trade Union' in the near future. Nor indeed will there be 'international bargaining' (except in a very few specialised sectors such as possibly over aviation) for quite a number of years. But the developments at ITS level indicate that the Trade Secretariats could begin to possess a flexibility and a responsiveness which match the responsiveness of a multinational management side.

There are of course continuing and formidable problems in the way of such coordination and the creation of such a flexible and agreed approach among the international trade union movement.

There are the basic *political* problems of various conflicts and ideologies of different parts of the movement. Hopefully, as this is being written, these problems are being resolved within Western Europe. The European Trade Union Congress now includes within it not only ICFTU-affiliated unions but also one major Communist-dominated union and all of the European World Council of Labour Unions. This is a major step forward and hopefully a final break with the traditions of the Cold War and the church-versus-state legacy of the early part of this century. When this is reflected at national level, political differences may become less marked. Unfortunately the differences between unions in Western Europe and those in the United States seem to be greater than they were in the recent past, and a considerable amount of breach mending between Europe and the AFL/CIO is urgently needed.

Then there are the basic *legal* differences. Any attempt at international coordinated industrial action runs immediately into a large number of legal snags. The international company does not have a single national or international corporate identity. Any sympathy strike against another subsidiary is therefore a strike, in law, against a third party. In most countries this kind of industrial action is either totally illegal or less protected than the direct form of industrial action. Hence any solidarity, even the banning of overtime, strictly runs the risk of legal redress in most Western countries. This situation is also the case in the UK where the Industrial Relations Act of 1971 substantially strengthened the law in this respect.[14] Unfortunately the recent Parliamentary manoeuvrings over the Labour Government's Trade Union and Labour Relations Bill, have virtually reinstated that part of the Tory Act.

There are also the basic *constitutional* difficulties referred to earlier. Trade unions are not only non-hierachical organisms, they are also anti-hierarchical and it is therefore difficult to impose a coordination from the international level, and indeed frequently at the national level.

One of the institutional difficulties in Western Europe — Britain in particular — is that the current collective bargaining machinery does not at present operate at company or group level. In the UK the bulk of collective bargaining is done at two levels: locally at *plant level*, particularly well developed in the engineering industry and other parts of the manufacturing industry where multinationals operate, such as chemicals, and then at *national level* through Joint Industrial Councils which cover a significant part of the firms within the industry. Hence within the subsidiaries of most multinational companies in the UK — whether British- or foreign-owned the substantive bargaining is done either at plant level or at national level (where the multinational company is only part of the employer's side). The full-time union officials therefore also operate at these two levels, and only rarely at the level of the company. Company-level negotiations about pensions, future plans, and so on are relatively recent and relatively rare. This makes it difficult for British trade unions to link up with their opposite numbers on a company basis. There has, of course, been an increasing tendency towards company bargaining within the UK, and this development is intensifying. Company-level machinery is beginning to be built up, both by 'combine level' shop stewards committees, and by full-time officials. But the fact remains that there is still a substantial gap at *national* level for a focus for trade union activity — let alone at international level. Nevertheless there has, of course, been an increasing tendency towards company bargaining within the UK.

Most fundamental of all, is the obvious but unpalatable fact that the interests of one worker in one plant of a company cannot always be readily explained as being identical as those of a worker in a distant country. It must be admitted that the most impressive of the moves towards international solidarity are not without a very strong element of self-interest. For instance, the desire of American unions to raise wages in America so that industry will not shift from America to Latin America and similarly the attitude of British unions towards wages in European-owned electronics companies in South-East Asia. Thus a humanitarian desire to raise the costs of wages to the company in South-East Asia coincides with the interest of Western labour in protecting jobs. But it would be too cynical to assume that all the concern of the international union movement

at the blatant exploitation of workers in these areas is on this sort
of level.

The Political Dimension

Though progress on the industrial relations dimension has been less
than dramatic, it should be recalled that the trade unions have at the
same time been extremely active on political fronts. As a result of
the 1971 World Congress of the ICFTU a joint ICFTU/ITS working
party was established. This working party immediately defined
ten areas of research, each of which reveals the political aspect of
the trade unions concerned:

(a) economic and political impact of multinational companies in
developing countries;
(b) multinational companies and European dictatorship countries;
(c) repercussions of multinational activities on employment;
(d) obstacles to industrial democracy posed by multinational
companies;
(e) social effects of incentives to attract foreign investment granted
by 'host' countries;
(f) overseas investment guarantee schemes by 'parent' countries;
their use as a lever controlling the behaviour of multinationals;
(g) the legal aspects of possibilities of trade union action across
frontiers;
(h) the effect of multinational companies on the world monetary
system;
(i) the possibility of drafting a detailed 'Code of Conduct' for
multinational companies;
(j) consideration of the possibility of drawing up a 'black-list'
for multinationals which fail to observe such standards.

The affiliates of both the ICFTU and the International Trade
Secretariats have been pursuing many of these points with their
individual national governments. As far as the TUC is concerned
one of the major areas of immediate interest has been the
conditions imposed on incoming private investment. The TUC
have insisted that before multinationals come to this country they

113

should undertake to observe British industrial relations practices. Broadly speaking, this has now been accepted by the new Labour Government as one of the 'strings' attached to inward investment (which of course itself attracts government subsidies). Unfortunately, the ability of the trade union movement within the *developing* countries to insist on criteria which would given them similar rights to British workers are extremely limited. The TUC has therefore also urged that overseas investments by British-owned companies should be sanctioned only if the company undertakes to observe basic ILO conventions in the country in which it is investing.

Of all the capital exporting countries, only Sweden has attempted to impose any kind of qualifications to overseas investments which relate to the bahaviour of multinational companies in their host country.

The TUC attempts to insist that it is the parent company's responsibility to try and impose such sanctions on the multinationals. Unfortunately the changed relationship which the growth of multinationals represents means that in most cases the nation-state cannot afford to alienate the management of even its 'own' multinationals too much, and hence over-insistence on the way they behave in South Africa or the Far East is not a great priority as far as governments are concerned. Nevertheless it would appear that the activities of the TUC and others in relation to the behaviour of British multinationals abroad, is beginning to have its effect. The insistence on ILO conventions in Hong Kong at this year's TUC is but one aspect of this.

The political impact of the trade union movement is exerted also in international agencies; the obvious one is the *International Labour Office*. There at the end of 1972 a working party was established including representatives of the TUC and other national centres, the ITSs and the WFTU unions to study the social effect of multinationals. The preliminary work done identifies a number of problems, particularly in the developing countries, and the work is now directed to creating a Code of Conduct, which will, amongst other things, give the right to representation of workers.

The pressure of the international movement is also visible within the *OECD*, despite the slow-moving nature of that organisation. Again the aim is to provide some form of Code of Practice, and also to identify the dis-economies of the 'Auction of Incentives' given by both developed and developing countries in order to attract foreign inward investment. The activities of these international agencies are often resented by many multinationals, though other of their representatives believe that a Code of Conduct is what is required, in order to offset the unfavourable propoganda directed at them by the trade unions and left-wing governments.

The influence of the trade union movement is also evident within the *European Commission*. Stemming from the Treaty of Rome, the main emphasis of the Commission's activity in this field in the past has been on removing barriers to the movement of capital and of labour and of creating a genuinely free trade common market, where resources as well as goods can travel across frontiers. The effect of this has been greatly to facilitate operations of multinationals at international mergers. There has been more recently a distinct change of tone within the Commission of Brussels, partly induced by trade union pressure, which now recognises the very urgent problems of controlling the multinationals which the reduction of trade and non-trade barriers has helped to nurture. It is likely that the next phase of the EEC's industrial policy — whether the UK is still a member or not — will be directed at the control of these powerful decision-makers. At the regional level at least, the EEC is the one supra-national authority which could potentially act as a major countervailing force to the enhanced power of the multinationals.

A number of European trade unions recognise this potential and it is perhaps time that the TUC saw involvement in Europe in these global and strategic terms.

The most authoritative analysis of the activities of the multinationals has been the publication in June 1974 of the report of the United Nations 'Group of Eminent Persons' on multinationals.[9] Unfortunately, there was not a representative of the trade unions on this body. Nevertheless the objective conclusions which that body came up with clearly reflected many of the trade union anxieties and substantiated some of those which had previously been queried.

115

The report notes that multinationals made only a marginal contribution towards solving the problems of world unemployment. And it notes that the great transnational flexibility of multinationals tilts the balance of bargaining power away from the local trade union to the multinational corporation. It therefore recommends greater participation of workers in the decision-making process for multinationals, and calls for international standards enforced by international collective bargaining on such matters as health and safety. It also urges that the law should be relaxed in relation to international solidarity strikes. More significantly the group recommended that 'home countries should prevent multinational companies going into countries where workers' rights are not respected, unless the affiliate obtains permission to apply internationally agreed labour standards, such as free collective bargaining and equal treatment of workers and human relations.' Despite its vagueness, this appears to mean the acceptance by the United Nations Advisory Body that parent countries should impose sanctions for their own multinationals to abide by ILO conventions.

Conclusions

It is always a dilemma for trade unions whether to pursue their objectives through the political and legislative process or through collective bargaining. In different countries a different balance has historically been drawn. With respect to multinational companies, it is clear that the writ of most nation-states is not sufficiently strong to control the multinationals. Therefore it is vital that some form of international countervailing power is mobilised. In the short term at least, the likelihood of international collective bargaining is extremely remote. Trade unions therefore are supporting efforts by the nation-states to get together, and to use the International Agencies that exist to offset the greatly enhanced power of multinationals.

Whether this will work remains to be seen. Whether there will in fact be international collective bargaining is also a matter of conjecture. What must be clear is that from the trade unions' own interests the two processes must work hand in hand. There is currently an argument going on between Charles Levison and certain elements within the Swedish LO.[15] The question at stake is whether it is desirable, let alone possible, for international collective bargaining to take place. Charles Levison is obviously very much in favour of this. He has stated 'that the aim is to increase rank and file solidarity on the national frontiers' and to organise the 'international contract and the coordinated international strike'. The Swedish argument is seen as an occasional expansion of national grievances in relation to multinational; these are valid tactics, but as an expression of the 'norm' in collective bargaining and in world power relations they are not. The development of international collective bargaining means that the trade union coordinating body is itself exercising an allocative function as between the various national trade union demands. This leads inevitably to trade unions becoming involved in issues far wider than collective bargaining itself.

Already decisions are made by the management of international companies (made to maximise global profits) which in practice vitally affect the international specialisation of labour. The growth in the international power of the trade union movement and the internationalisation of collective bargaining would increasingly involve unions in these decisions. The danger is that a pattern could emerge whereby wages and working conditions within multinational corporations in a given country became severely out of line with those in the rest of that particular economy. It is not desirable from the point of view of trade union organisations or the individual worker, that international collective bargaining should be uprooted from the national and local context.

On the one hand, therefore, trade unions need to develop a countervailing power. On the other, they must guard against the long-term effects of having created it. This is a question not only for trade unions, but also for governments and relations between government and industry. Multinational collective bargaining may well prove an advantage to the manager of multinational companies. It would probably both reduce the risks in multinational decision-taking and planning and provide a more stable environment for multinationals to operate. But by abstracting even further from the

117

national economic framework a development in this direction further undermines the ability of national economies to conduct planning within a stable framework. It is not in the interests of the trade union movement to develop the process to the extent that it has this destabilising effect on national economic management. Rather, the political aim of the trade unions must be almost the reverse: to influence and control the apparatus of the state to offset the power that multinationals possess and to minimise the regressive social changes that their decisions and activities may cause. It is a difficult tightrope for the leadership of the international trade union movement to walk.

NOTES

1. See *The Times*, 1 October 1970.
2. Charles Levinson, *Capital, Inflation and the Multinationals*, 1971.
3. TUC, *International Companies*, 1970.
4. D.J.C. Forsyth, *British Journal of Industrial Relations*, March 1973. Extract with J. Gennard and M.D. Steuer, *British Journal of Industrial Relations*, July 1971.
5. See relevant TUC Annual Reports.
6. For the most recent assessment of the situation in South Africa, see TUC Report, *Trade Unions in South Africa*, 1973.
7. G. Adam, 'New Trends in International Trade', World Wide Survey of De-dominiling (1970 Budapest), probably the most detailed analysis available.
8. *International Metalworkers Federation Study*, K. Casserini (unpublished, 1972).
9. UN Report, 1974.
10. AFL-CIO, February 1971 — Executive Statement.
11. ICFTU, 'The Multinational Challenge 1971'.
12. Various ICF Journals, 1973.
13. D. Gallin, Nijmegen Conference, 1973.
14. For details, see monograph, K.W. Wedderburn, *Multinational Enterprises and National Labour Law*, 1972.
15. Charles Levinson the LO, 1974, published by LO, Sweden.

APPENDIX

International Trade Union Organisations

Confederations

ICFTU	International Confederation of Free Trade Unions. Affiliates are the national centres (i.e. TUC's) of broadly non-communist socialist orientation. Main affiliates TUC and DGB (Germany). It currently excludes American AFL/CIO. Headquarters Brussels.
WFTU	World Federation of Trade Unions. Communist-dominated unions' confederation of national centres. Includes East European unions, plus CGT (France), CGIL (Italy) and unions Latin American and Asia. Affiliates: Headquarters Prague.
WCL	World Confederation of Labour: Confederation of National Centres formerly of communist allegiance. Main strength of France (CFDT) Belgium and Netherlands. Headquarters Paris.
ETUC	European Trade Union Confederation: Confederation of national centres in Western Europe. Cover EEC plus rest of Western Europe. Includes all ECFTU affiliated national centres, and all WCL affiliates in Western Europe plus Irish CTU. The CGIL (Communist-dominated, Italy) has recently joined. Headquarters Brussels.

Trade Secretariats (ITS)

These are confederations of individual unions on an industrial basis. They consist almost entirely of unions affiliated to ICFTU national centres, plus the Americans. The equivalent organisation on the

119

WFTU side are generally known as Trade International (TI's).

The main ITS's in the context of multinationals are as follows:

ICF	International Federation of Chemical & General Workers (covering Processing Industries).
IMF	International Metalworkers Federation (Engineering, Metal Manufacture, Shipbuilding Vehicles).
IUF	International Foodworkers (Food, Tobacco, Hotels, Catering).
ITGWF	International Tailor, Garment and Leather Workers Federation.
ITF	International Transport Workers Federation.
IFPAAW	International Federation of Plantation, Agricultural and Allied Workers
IFPCW	International Federation of Petroleum and Chemical Workers (Oil and Petro-chemicals — some overlap with ICF; it is likely the two will shortly merge).
FIET	International White Collar and Technical Workers.

National Centres

TUC	Trades Union Congress
DGB	Deutsche Gewerkschaftsbund
CGT	France (Communist) Confederation Generale du Travail
CFDT	Christian Federation du Travail
FO	Force Ouvrière
CGIL	Confederazione General Italiana del Lavoro
CSIL	Confederazione Socialistiche Italian del Lavoro
UIL	Union Italiana del Lavoro
AFI/CIO	American Federation of Labor-Confederation Organisation

5. THE MANAGEMENT OF INDUSTRIAL RELATIONS IN A CHANGING ENVIRONMENT

Andrew W. Gottschalk

Introduction

This chapter has three separate but closely intertwined tasks. The first is to provide a brief account and analysis of some of the major changes in British industrial relations during the past decade. The second is to develop a framework which links the contributions of four authors who display a diversity of approach towards the theme of industrial relations in a changing environment. The third is to predict directions in which British industrial relations may develop over the foreseeable future and tentatively to suggest how the managements of companies might respond. In doing this, to a considerable extent I build upon a foundation provided by my fellow contributors, and this has influenced the direction of my own ideas. Some of the ideas and points of view presented by Sir Leonard Neal and Mr. Alan Fisher, both concerned with recent British experiences, will be incorporated in the first section. Mr. Adrian Cadbury's paper on participation in UK management will be discussed in the middle section which seeks to explore some of the issues requiring our attention in the very near future. Finally, Mr. Larry Whitty's paper on the trade union response to the multinational company forms a cornerstone of the final section, concerned with exploring some of the implications of future trends in industrial relations.

Voluntarism in British industrial relations has declined in the last ten years.[1] It can be taken alternatively to mean a preference for collective bargaining over any form of state regulation, a desire to keep industrial disputes out of the courts and maintain a non-legalistic form of collective agreement, or an insistence on the parties to collective agreements having complete autonomy in their conclusion. The attempts of successive Labour and Conservative Governments since 1964 to develop prices and incomes policies and the introduction of the Industrial Relations Act in 1971 were deliberately

121

aimed blows at voluntarism. Their implications for the management of industrial relations will be analysed to show the effect within the company and in the larger national framework. As the attempts to develop a prices and incomes policy precede the 1971 Industrial Relations Act, it would be useful to begin there. The social, political and economic framework in which the Conservative Government subsequently passed the Act had already been considerably altered by the earlier and partly successful attempt to run a prices and incomes policy and the Labour Government's aborted Industrial Relations Bill.

The Productivity Agreement Phase

The Labour Government's incomes policy lasted approximately four years, from 1965 to 1969. During most of this period, trade unions could only secure a substantial wage increase for their members by concluding a plant productivity agreement. This in itself might be regarded as a major contribution of incomes policy, but its most important feature was that it encouraged managements to take an initiative in the conduct of workplace industrial relations. The symptoms of drift and inertia became plain; low productivity, long hours of overtime, a large gap between rates and take-home pay, etc., etc. As Allan Flanders suggested:

'In conditions of full employment the only viable alternative to . . . a disastrous policy of drift is for management to engage in a new type of creative workplace bargaining, of which the existing examples of 'productivity bargaining' offer valuable prototypes . . . Such bargaining is not only creative in the sense that it contributes to higher productivity, it also serves to create new social relations in industry in which it is possible for the participants to act responsibly.'[2]

Managements faced three broad strategies to deal seriously with low productivity. They could be very cautious and only seek to buy out bad practices. Existing arrangements which impeded productivity were identified, their costs evaluated. They were then

122

bought out by management. A second approach, which required
more commitment by both managers and trade union representatives,
was a gain-sharing strategy. Here a broad formula was developed to
link changes in earnings and hours of work to improved performance
of specific work groups. The third, which required the development
of an organisational perspective, placed industrial relations quite
firmly in the larger context of the organisation's daily operation;
increased effectiveness did not merely start and finish on the
shop-floor. What this approach involved was clearly seen by a senior
Alcan manager in describing his Company's experiences in the
negotiation of the Rogerstone productivity agreement.[3] He pointed
out that:

> 'industrial relations problems may exist in an organisational
> context and that they may be accentuated by other structural
> defects and that unless these are tackled, any action on the
> industrial relations front is at best a short-term palliative
> and at worst a waste of time.'

He then said:

> 'When we were approached by the PIB, we discussed with
> them at the outset of their Inquiry whether, in fact we
> should be included in their reference at all. We did this because
> we thought that the PIB were only looking at the industrial
> relations aspects of a reorganisation of which the agreement with
> the Unions was in fact only one part. We felt strongly, in line
> with a number of theories of social organisation of industry,
> that although you can pick one area of industrial relations
> activity to study, such as productivity bargaining, an isolated
> treatment begs too many questions.'

The architects of incomes policy deliberately sought to link
national policy to the daily conduct of workplace industrial
relations. The main instrument was the National Board for Prices
and Incomes. In its first General Report covering the period
April 1965 to July 1966, NBPI noted that judging particular
cases fulfilled three purposes:

> 'First, to bring home to the parties immediately concerned
> in a reference to the implications of their actions for others . . .

secondly, going beyond the parties immediately concerned in a reference to bring home to others the wiser implications of their actions; thirdly, in the longer term to promote a quicker adaptation of past practices to new needs.'[4]

This was NBPI's approach during its whole existence. It suggests that a statutory incomes policy, if combined with an appropriate investigating agency, need not stifle management initiatives in the conduct of industrial relations.

Productivity bargaining itself went through three distinct phases. The first, beginning at Fawley in 1960, lasted until the summer of 1967 when the NBPI produced its first report on productivity agreements. The second lasted only two years. During this time a vast number of deals were negotiated, which by June 1969 had encompassed 25 per cent of all employed workers. Nor, as some early critics suggested, were these agreements confined to capital-intensive industries. As Brian Towers noted, 'by the end of 1969 productivity agreements, however modest, were present in virtually every branch of the economy.'[5] These two years, the high water mark of productivity bargaining, were the direct result of 'the emphasis placed on the productivity criterion in the current productivity, prices and incomes policy.'[6] The NBPI may have been too self-congratulatory, but it is quite clear that without the backing of incomes policy and a supportive agency, such bargaining could not and would not survive. Towards the end of 1969 erosion of incomes policy was already being gradually eroded. Paradoxically productivity bargaining continued momentum in sectors where it was apparently more difficult to apply, such as some local and central government services. Essentially, with the collapse of incomes policy, productivity bargaining disappeared. The Labour Government failed to work for an effective policy beyond the end of 1969. To attribute this to the pressures for electoral success is an over-simplification. Income policy collapsed because there was a vast gap between the anticipated benefits and the reality of what took place. That this gap existed and that it affected trade union attitudes towards incomes policy is pointed out by Alan Fisher:[7]

'Even allowing for our scepticism the events of the last two

years have left us disturbed . . . time and again our expectations
have been frustrated.'
Other areas of social and fiscal policy appeared to be out of phase.
Thus Alan Fisher quotes Alex Jarratt's comment that:

'Attempting to apply this view of the past to the future,
I think there can be no question of reintroducing a formal
incomes policy in isolation. It has to be part of an overall
approach to economic and social improvement, to be
in some way a positive policy.'[8]

A gradual but systematic increase in unemployment made trade
unions more reluctant to change work practices which might reduce
job opportunities. Only where directly or indirectly the Government was
the employer, and where serious shortages existed, did productivity
bargaining survive; and then not for more than eighteen months. By
mid-1971 it could safely be said that productivity agreements were
obsolete. Those still operating were now two or three years old.

Attempts at Legislative Reform

When the Conservatives won in June 1970 it was quite clear that
voluntarism, already under pressure from prices and incomes policy,
was now going to be directly challenged by legislation based upon
the policy statement 'Fair Deal at Work'.[9] The objectives, eventually
contained in the Industrial Relations Act, can be summarised as:
(1) setting standards for good industrial relations;
(2) safeguarding those who conform to them;
(3) protecting individual rights;
(4) providing new methods of resolving industrial disputes which
     would curtail strike action.
These policy objectives arose out of an analysis of industrial relations
and the experience of the previous Labour Government. Sir Leonard
Neal in Chapter 1 clearly identifies factors which influenced the
architects of the Act and describes the new philosophy. There existed
disquiet about both the scale and intensity of industrial conflict in
our society. He notes that:

'The strike has, somehow, acquired a morality of its own

125

which appears to make any interruption of work justifiable, irrespective of its purposes and heedless of its methods. The "right" to strike in some instances has been elevated to such a status and it has been talked about and stressed to such an extent by the few that the two words have become confused and a strike becomes "right" merely because it is a strike.'[10]
The Act and the events surrounding its introduction and operation were, however very different from those its sponsors had intended. This can mainly be attributed to the Act's implicit analysis of the causes of industrial conflict. Its correctness was challenged both then and now by critics of the Industrial Relations Act. As Sir Leonard Neal observes, the diagnosis is not agreed: 'nevertheless some factors seem to be significant . . . while others are incidental . . . All seem to have come together at about the same point in time.'[11]

He lists five origins of increased industrial conflicts: the paradox of affluence, the interdependence of industrial production, the intellectual apologia for conflict, the abdication of authority, and the failure of collective bargaining. He notes:
'one of the strangest phenomena of the world of post-war affluence . . . the virtues of conflict . . . are extolled. Conflict, we are told, is necessary . . . out of the clash of interests and will new ideas and new orders will develop.'[12]
Unfortunately he did not distinguish the various types of conflict, such as distributive, structural and human relations, each of which requires from management a different response. Without necessarily being aware of it the unitary frame of reference was gradually being discarded by many managements. This meant that they ceased to perceive the organisation as a structure in which there was one source of authority, one set of legitimate goals identified by the most senior managers and that conflict was therefore the result of a breakdown in communication. Productivity bargaining and a realisation of the practical benefits of a pluralistic frame of reference had begun to create a new situation. Managers had now recognised that within any organisation there exist a number of

different groups each with different interests, goals and values. Their task was to build a consensus which would allow the organisation to achieve its overall objectives through internal negotiation and consultation. Sir Leonard Neal then points out: 'A more benign management view would seek to enlarge the areas of joint regulation and responsibility at the shop-floor level.'[13]
So he is a reluctant pluralist!

More managements were quite unwilling to rock the boat by demanding legally binding collective agreements. The phrase 'This is not a legally binding agreement' was reduced to a mnemonic TINLEA and repeated everywhere. The Act generated for most managements an enormous administrative overload, such as issuing revised Contracts of Employment, which effectively prevented any other initiative in the field of industrial relations. Other aspects of the Government's economic and social policy had also radically altered the negotiating climate. The comprehensive plant procedure agreement favoured by the Donovan Commission and the Commission on Industrial Relations lived but briefly. The effort required to negotiate such major procedural changes, as for example at the Delta Metal Company in Birmingham,[14] were left unsupported in the political climate generated, however unintentionally, by the Act. Managements which had earlier shown initiative in plant bargaining found it more difficult and were apparently satisfied to pursue a successful policy of containment. As one senior industrial relations specialist commented:

'We got our pay and productivity agreement in time for it to have been influenced by Incomes Policy and now we will administer it and obtain our long-term objectives which are to stabilise our labour costs and increase our profitability. If this is to happen, we also have to hope and pray that this Act passes us by. I don't care about the token stoppages but I won't fight a politician's battle for him.'

This gap between political rhetoric and industrial relations practice was also clearly seen in the closed shop issue. According to the Act it was to disappear except in some very clearly defined circumstances but as the Commission on Industrial Relations pointed out: 'As in

127

1972 informal post-entry closed shops continued to operate almost unaltered in many companies . . .'[15], many managers felt they were being drawn into a political conflict not of their choosing and which might in the long run prove to be dysfunctional. Even if as individuals they perceived merit in the Act, many were suprised by the determined and united opposition of the trade union movement. They now saw a conflict between government and organised labour which seemed irrelevant to the problems of running a business. Trade union activity at the national level was primarily concerned with maintaining the momentum of political opposition to the Act and in all but a few instances the effects of this campaign did not reach the workplace. There, the pattern of industrial relations continued in the form so accurately described by Allan Flanders as 'largely informal, largely fragmented and largely autonomous'.

Although the Act remained on the Statute Book until the Labour Government repealed many of its provisions in the middle of 1974, the objectives of its architects were almost totally unrealised. The attitudes and behaviour it sought to influence remained virtually unchanged. The Act, coming on top of other decisions about social and fiscal policy, resulted in hardening trade union attitudes. The slogan 'free collective bargaining' had acquired a face validity and was accepted, as Sir Leonard Neal points out, with 'a childlike faith' which had little to do with the complexities of industrial relations in a changing economic, social and political environment. Events were, however, forcing the Government to reconsider the utility of reintroducing some form of prices and incomes policy. The CBI 'price initiative' in August 1971 was a very useful and sincere contribution to the attack on the mounting inflationary pressures. Unfortunately, hopes that the trade unions would respond to the CBI action by restraining wage demands voluntarily were not realised. Whether this hope was ever realistic is doubtful, for the Act had soured relations between the Conservative Government and trade union movement. The CBI initiative lasted twelve months, until July 1972. From then until October 1972 it continued mainly as a daily reminder of the CBI's political sophistication and maturity.

Problems of Incomes Policy

During that Autumn, however, it became increasingly obvious that events were forcing the Conservative administration to reconsider its previous rejection of state intervention in collective bargaining. Tripartite talks between the Government, the CBI and the TUC, aimed at securing a voluntary system of pay and price controls, were almost certain to break down although they

'were notable for the large amount of Ministerial time which they absorbed, for the wide range of subjects they covered.'[16]

The problem of rebuilding a consensus was too great. The gap between the policies and philosophy of the Conservative Government and the TUC were too wide to be bridged in such a short but intensive period of talks. Nevertheless, as one participant noted 'the tripartite talks embodied the institutional analysis of inflation in its more uncompromising form.'[17]

With the collapse of these talks, the Conservative Government found itself with no viable policy alternative and was forced to introduce a 90-day standstill on pay and prices. This decisive action, after what looked like a period of inactivity and weakness, was greeted with general public relief. Apparently the Government had created time which could be used to put right past mistakes and to develop a sophisticated policy capable of preventing some of the worst iniquities and distortions associated with the previous Labour Government's prices and incomes policy.

From November 1972 what was in effect a two-pronged attack on voluntarism was under way. The first prong, the Act, had if nothing else, some political credibility and consistency. The second prong, statutory prices and incomes policy, had a large measure of public acceptance but was resisted, and actively rejected where it mattered, by the trade union movement. The Conservative policy, once undertaken, was subsequently defended and justified to the bitter end. No political party since the war has adopted as its main election plank a policy to which it was reluctantly driven half-way through its period of office. Unfortunately, it was not sufficiently appreciated how prices and incomes policies, highly fragile instruments, depend upon active endorsement from both sides of industry. The Act had effectively destroyed the basis for consensus. It was now almost too easy for the defenders of voluntarism to extend their campaign from demanding the repeal of the Act to abolishing the Pay Board.

For individual companies, the new legislation presented a number of quite serious difficulties. The Pay and Price Code was in some ways much more sophisticated than any of its predecessors. The drafting was more precise and had a greater cutting edge. Managers and shop stewards found their areas of discretion, said to be so vital in plant bargaining, effectively reduced. For example where productivity and restructuring schemes were implemented the Code required 'that no such increases may be implemented with effect from a date earlier than 28th February 1973; that thereafter such increases may be implemented 90 days after their due date provided this is not less than 12 months after the previous settlement.'[18] Fortunately for them, the Conservative Government were able to reassemble a highly competent team of civil servants at the Pay Board under the able leadership of Derek Robinson, the Oxford labour economist and statistician, its Deputy Chairman. The NBPI's disappearance in April 1971 had not resulted in the permanent loss of its expertise. The Pay Board's senior staff had a wealth of experience and insight immediately to draw on. The Board's advisory report on Anomalies is clearly sophisticated analytically and understood the problems of implementing a statutory policy. Having established the criterion to qualify as an anomaly the Board point out that:

> 'the number of major cases to qualify at the national level would not be large although there may be a large number of small cases spread throughout industry and commerce. We estimate the monetary sum involved in remedying the anomaly in full for all known cases would amount to 0.06 per cent of the national wage bill, or 0.1 per cent making allowance for unknown cases mainly at plant and company level.'[19]

This precision and depth of analysis were to be the Pay Board's hallmark. Yet a problem remained unresolved. To be successful, an incomes policy must link the activities of the individual enterprise clearly to the larger national scene. The NBPI criteria used in the assessment of productivity bargaining encouraged management initiatives in collective bargaining. Many such deals adopted a joint gain approach, or what has been described as 'integrative bargaining'.[20] The Government's incomes policy was too rigid. The new policy placed the manager in the front line with no room for manoeuvre. The norm immediately became the minimum settlement point. Bargaining tactics appeared to regress to 'win-lose' or 'distributive bargaining',[21] in which the parties were more concerned to maintain their shares rather than increase the total sum available. The Pay Code did nothing to encourage the more effective of human resources. Unions reluctantly accepted settlements within the norm but conceded nothing to their managements. It may even be argued that, as it did not link increases in productivity to increases in earnings, the norm was too high for certain sectors of the economy, and that it further weakened the financial position of companies, thus placing future employment prospects in jeopardy. Probably the harshest critique of the Pay Code is contained in the researches of Hilde Behrend:

> 'The code would thus appear to be divisive, loaded towards sectional claims and self-interest and this would widen the range of negotiated as opposed to the intended range of pay increase differentials. Such a process is dangerous because instead of decelerating pay increase expectations it could lead to increased frustration among those who feel left behind, and therefore to renewed agitation for higher pay increase amounts giving a further twist to inflation.'[22]

The Conservative Government's incomes policy collapsed in the face of the second miners' strike and the resulting three-day-week. In retrospect, it lacked insight in its preparation and sophistication and judgement in its application. Incomes policy was basically at variance with Conservative political philosophy; it was seen only as a tool of economic management. For this government it was not, as Sir Leonard Neal comments in his chapter, 'a repudiation of the capitalistic ethic to assert that, from time to time, the most extreme excesses of the market should yield to the restraints of the community law . . .'[23]

It is possible, as has been shown by Barbara Wootton, to criticise the consequences of collective bargaining,[24] in particular in terms of its effects on the unorganised and the poor. The defence of differentials also in part implies certain assumptions about their value. Any attempt to apply even a rough and ready concept of 'fairness' or 'social justice' to collective bargaining will almost certainly fail. But the two-pronged attack on voluntarism as the salient characteristic of British collective bargaining failed because it was essentially negative. The Act and the Pay Code offered no alternative, no hope. Collective bargaining was isolated from its social, economic and political context.

In the decade since 1964 voluntarism, the principal characteristic of British collective bargaining, has come under almost continuous attack. It has emerged, superficially at least, virtually unscathed. The return of a Labour Government in February 1974 implied the Government's acceptance of voluntarism. Even if they only wanted peace and quiet and an end of the three-day-week, most people were aware that the Labour Party based its claim to power on the quality of its relationship with the trade union movement, something which apparently clearly differentiated it from the Conservative Party. In the previous months the Labour Party and the trade union movement had thoroughly reappraised the objectives and achievements of their relationship. This stock-taking had two aims; to analyse past mistakes and to develop a joint approach in which, with a Labour Government, a sound working relationship could be based on trust and cooperation. The resulting social contract has a number of characteristics. First, it recognises voluntarism as salient in British collective bargaining. The Labour Party therefore committed itself to repeal the Industrial Relations Act. Second, it placed collective bargaining within the framework of government social and economic policies. If at a future date a Labour Government were to reassess the need for an incomes policy it could at least be argued that having recognised the context in which it would have to be placed it might have a better chance

132

of success. Finally, the social contract could be said to have encouraged and further strengthened the supports of responsible voluntarism. In one sense it represented the 'last chance'. As Alan Fisher comments:

'Whatever reluctance there may be in some other quarters, the trade union movement recognises that political considerations — *and* political actions by Government — a major factor in determining the character of industrial relations. Our argument is not that there should be no government intervention, but what the nature of that intervention should be and what the policy objectives of Government are in making that intervention.'[25]

If it now fails the alternatives are grim. Unfortunately, the Labour Government has not yet been able to build with the CBI and employers in general, the relationship it has with the TUC. Use of such tripartite machinery as exists, in particular NEDO, may result in tripartite national economic planning and management but this will probably take at least another twelve months. As Sir Leonard Neal also notes 'The TUC and the CBI have a standing and a responsibility in the community that requires and deserves consultation. An on-going dialogue about the nature of the social and economic problem is, therefore, essential.'[26]

The problems of inflation may well force cooperation from otherwise reluctant quarters in the same way that it may force a modification in the rate of implementation of the Labour Government's electoral manifesto.

Innovation in Collective Bargaining

British industrial relations have been dominated for the last ten years by the two issues of incomes policy and industrial relations legislation. We should not however assume that literally nothing else of significance has taken place. Throughout the decade a number of issues have arisen, some of only a brief life, for example 'flexi-time'. Others continue to be of long term significance and to these I now turn. They are: the use of information to collective bargaining and the extension of the bargaining agenda, a reappraisal

133

of the facilities for conciliation and arbitration, the impact of growing
unionisation amongst white-collar and managerial employees, and the
challenge of resolving the problem of minority group relations at the
workplace. Mr. Adrian Cadbury has raised many of these issues in his
paper but as a bridge to this, it is appropriate to take up a point raised
by Sir Leonard Neal:

> 'And one way that might be considered for achieving the
> maximum degree of freedom in collective bargaining is to see
> whether we can construct a national system of conciliation
> and arbitration by isolating the factors that appear to
> contribute more than others to the volatility of collective
> bargaining.
>
> It seems that these factors include a widespread confusion
> about the facts in the arguments of both sides . . .'[27]

He then goes on to suggest that:

> 'independent fact-finders should be appointed whose task
> it would be "to determine the facts with the parties". Such
> a method might allow the public interest to be involved
> at a much earlier stage in wage bargains and would not
> exclude . . . the Government of the day from indicating what
> its concept of the year's norm or maximum for increases
> in incomes should be.'[28]

Here indeed is a challenge for both sides of industry! It is, however,
vital to distinguish between two "fact-finding' situations. The first,
to which we have in part become accustomed, is the investigatory
work of Courts of Inquiry and more recently the reports of the
Commission on Industrial Relations. Here one has been concerned
with a statutory agency whose task it has been to facilitate
improvements in the quality of collective bargaining where the
negotiating parties

> 'can be materially assisted by a third party able to offer a
> wide range of experience, impartial advice, the opportunity
> for informal discussion, and new methods of inquiry and
> analysis designed to help the parties see their problem in
> a new light.'[29]

The value of this work, in the middle and long term, is beyond

134

doubt. For example the CIR report on International Harvester Co. was followed by considerable improvements in the company's effectiveness in both purely financial terms but also more significantly in the quality of its industrial relations. A second type of fact-finding situation would involve attempting to influence the bargaining process before 'opinions have hardened and uncompromising attitudes have been struck'. This is obviously a much more difficult task but should not be lightly dismissed merely on this account. In order to explore its potential value it is necessary to analyse a case study. I choose the annual ICI wage negotiations for convenience and because they comply with one of Sir Leonard's criteria:

> 'wage bargaining patterns tend to be established during each
> annual wage round . . . and even within industries a similar
> tendency exists for one company . . . to be the pace-setter.'[30]

The ICI negotiations also clearly illustrate the attempt by trade unions to gradually but systematically extend the agenda for collective bargaining.

Productivity bargaining has put the traditional limitation of the annual wage round to a discussion of wages and hours of work under considerable pressure. A number of trade unions, and in particular the TGWU and the GMWU, have used their experience of productivity bargaining at the plant and industry level to demand a fuller disclosure of information by management and to extend the agenda for negotiation. Where managements adopted an integrative strategy in productivity bargaining, they had to be prepared to increase both the scale and the quality of information given to trade union representatives. The NBPI in its first report adopted as essentially cautious approach . . .

> 'Clearly undertakings must be prepared to release more
> information than is normal in conventional negotiations
> if they are to win the confidence of the unions for this
> novel type of agreement and if they are to reach a successful
> settlement. We do not suggest, however, that all relevant
> information should be made available to trade union
> representatives, or indeed that the latter would necessarily
> wish this. Such facts might give the unions precise information

135

on what employers could pay before he had any notion of the figure for which they were prepared to settle. To decide whether and when to release this information is part of the art of negotiations, and unions as well as companies have their own differing styles of negotiation.'[31]

The CIR in their report subsequently suggested that
'Management should formulate a considered policy on the subject of disclosure. Such a policy should aim to be as open and helpful as possible in meeting trade union needs.'[32]

In April 1971 at the ICI annual wage round the unions representing the employees covered by the Weekly Staff Agreement (the company's productivity deal) submitted a claim. They argued this was a natural development from their joint involvement in productivity bargaining. But there were also some new departures . . .
'We are therefore not today putting to you just a wage claim in the traditional sense. We are putting to you a comprehensive proposal . . . which goes well beyond the previously expressed managerial notions of productivity bargaining . . . We set out to restore our members' faith in productivity bargaining – and in current circumstances that is a major task! . . . We shall have a look at problems which have implications well beyond the confines of ICI . . . We shall be talking about the relationship between real earnings growth, costs and capacity utilisation. We shall examine the connections between productivity, investment and unemployment.'[33]

The union lodged a monetary claim and presented a case for extending the WSA to provide opportunities for greater participation.
'In this context we have decided quite unequivocally to increase our participation role as trade unionists and as members of the public in ICI's corporate planning. . .'[34]

and for changes in job evaluation methods, for the provision of control data on the cost savings attributatble to improved labour efficiency 'to establish mutuality in access to and analysis of the relevant control and cost data.'[35]

This lengthy and wide-ranging claim brought the following reply

136

from the management:

> 'The Unions have presented the Company with a detailed
> and lengthy document. Included in it are many matters we
> would not normally expect to find in a weekly staff
> salary claim. Much thought has obviously been given to
> the arguments and supporting data, and in this response,
> the Company has set out to answer in detail both the
> economic case for salary increases and the more
> philosophical points you make related to wider issues of
> personnel policy.'[36]

The company's opening statement was equally detailed and it clearly
identified two different areas of disagreement. The first was
substantive, i.e. the amount the company could afford to pay etc.,
and the second was philosophical. (Sir Leonard Neal's proposal
would only influence the area of substantive disagreement, leaving
the 'philosophical' issue unresolved, in many ways the most
important.) The unions noted:

> 'Having completed the monetary area of our demands we
> wish to add a philosophical postscript. It is sometimes argued
> that collective bargaining is only concerned with gross pay
> and that it is for Parliament alone to decide on the real
> social wage. We are sure that you as progressive employers,
> will reject any such limitation upon the scope of collective
> bargaining . . .'[37]

They therefore suggested that the concept of real disposable
purchasing power be used in negotiations, i.e. a net figure.
This the unions would argue could protect their members
earnings against the effect of inflation. The company's rejection
of this idea was presented in fairly blunt terms.

> 'First, it is the sum of gross pay that will affect ICI's
> profits and capacity to grow. Second, how in any
> practical way could the Company make equitable
> judgements about the right social wage for single men,
> married men . . . men with ten children . . . Even if this
> approach were acceptable to the Company – which it is
> not – what do the Unions do when tax is reduced by the

137

Government to increase the disposable incomes of their members? Give the Company's increase back?'[38]

Sir Leonard suggests that certain facts can be objectively established. Yet at the heart of the union's wage claim at ICI is a difference about methods of accounting and the interpretation of complex data. In the elegance of the idea is its limitation. Data for collective bargaining is interpreted and communicated to win a particular case. The bargaining process might be helped by objectivity but this is in itself an assumption. In the ICI situation the parties arrived at a settlement and it is doubtful how far it was influenced by the type of claim presented. The negotiating process includes its accusations of bad faith, barbed comments and false indignation. Some participants might even suggest that this is an essential ingredient. For example when two years later the trade unions again took up the theme of their informational needs they noted 'a real advance in ICI's approach' and that . . .

'As we will demonstrate later . . . the trade union side
has been able to gain an unprecedented amount of
information and over-view of pay among ICI employees
by putting the New Earnings Survey returns provided by
the Company on computer. In this way valuable information,
which the Company has hitherto neglected, is made available
to both sides (we don't intend to have double standards on
information disclosure and will make all the relevant
information, including computer print-outs, available to ICI
if the Company wants it).'[39]

Quite clearly a somewhat tongue-in-cheek statement! The senior company spokesman's reply was direct and clear:

'Allow me to begin with a complaint. I do not make it in
any carping spirit, but because to me the nature of the
relationship which we have with you as Unions is a prime
consideration, I would be less than honest, and less than
dutiful to my own concern for how those relationships may
develop in the future, were I not to say now that some
aspects of your claim document – the tone and nature of
certain arguments in particular – I found difficult to accept
and irrelevant to your claim. . . . Nevertheless there are in

138

view passages, and even whole sections, in your claim which seem
to me to be designed more for display and to embarrass the
Company, rather than seriously to challenge us or help us better
to understand your views and claims as unions . . .

    As you know well, our view on these matters, whether it be
industrial democracy, information about the business, or
development in employment conditions, is that they are advanced
by serious and regular discussions . . . on a continuing and
evolutionary basis . . .'[40]

If the two negotiating parties, ICI and the unions, were jointly to seek
out an 'independent fact-finder', his chances of success might be good.
Such action might arise out of a developing and continually evolving
bargaining relationship, but I suspect this is fairly unlikely. In the
situation, however, which Mr. Adrian Cadbury describes, where
institutions for effective worker participation gradually develop, a
representative body of the employees might seek an 'independent
fact-finder' to clarify a particular problem. The value of Sir Leonard
Neal's idea may be in its application to support the development
of effective participation rather than as an attempt to influence the
bargaining process by facilitating an understanding of the
complexities of the information produced by companies for
employees elected to various internal bodies.

Building Effective Participation

In the first section of his paper, Adrian Cadbury deals with the
demand for participation. He lists changes in education,
communications, the nature of work and work-force composition
which must lead companies to consider the advantages of moving
towards schemes which encourage greater participation in
management. Unfortunately these changes have not had much
impact mainly because managers have been unwilling to
'have a go'. The more positive reason is

    ' . . . participation should therefore lead to better decisions and
to decisions that will command a greater degree of commitment
from those who have to implement them. This is a critical point

139

because the degree of single-mindedness with which a decision is put into action is usually more important than the quality of the decision itself.'[41]

This argument contrasts with which he describes as a 'defensive rather than a positive argument for participation' which is the concern for security and continuity of employment. Many recent British attempts to develop workable forms of industrial democracy have arisen out of crises; for example UCS and Meriden. One lesson is that unless sufficient time exists to allow for specific changes to be made in the structure and methods of working of the enterprise the chances of long-term success are very low. Here, German experience contrasts quite sharply with that of the UK. It has long operated in a different cultural and collective bargaining framework. Until quite recently many employers and trade unionists agreed that to 'transplant' the German system would be wrong. The TUC in its interim report on Industrial Democracy now notes that:

'The TUC attitude to existing European experiments is that their system of two-tier boards is probably a desirable development in that the structure gives workers' representatives a degree of joint control over all the major decisions of the company: closures, redundancy, major technological changes, mergers, etc.'[42]

Mr. Cadbury notes that one major obstacle to be overcome is the perceived threat to the existing pattern of management authority. It could be argued that a two-tier board system might help to legitimise a certain level of management authority which in part has been eroded by the existence of collective bargaining. On the other hand Mr. Cadbury does sound a note of caution:

'If the movement towards greater participation starts at the board level it is likely to raise the maximum expectations for the minimum results in the eyes of the ordinary employee, thus adding to the danger of disillusion. Secondly, for participation at board level to be effective it must be based on a participative structure which extends throughout the enterprise and the top of the pyramid is the wrong end from which to build such a structure.'[43]

140

Within the United Kingdom the major part of the discussion on developing various forms of participation in the management of the enterprise has focused on the shop-floor and trade union members. Adrian Cadbury points to an issue often overlooked, consciously or unconsciously, namely 'the position of management in the representative structure'. He

'would increasingly expect managers to become organised in a more formal way outside their professional associations and this will reinforce their claim to participate and make such participation administratively more straightforward.'[44]

It is almost an accepted 'fact of life' that the supervisor and other members of middle management are caught in a limbo. Once there they are conveniently forgotten until a crisis drives them into the arms of a trade union. Mr. Cadbury's acceptance of managerial unionisation is well in advance of the attitudes of other senior executives in British manufacturing companies and, even more, because it combines a coherent management philosophy with administrative rationality. Managerial unionisation has often been bitterly opposed by companies whose senior executives cling to a frame of reference inappropriate for the conduct of industrial relations. CIR's reports clearly indicate the problems associated with a company's failure to recognise unions which have successfully organised groups of managerial employees.

Two issues, however, remain unresolved: the types of decision in which people will want to participate and the potentially ambiguous position of senior executives. Mr. Cadbury suggests that

'there is a distinction between types of decision, which is worth pursuing one stage further in the context of participation . . . there are two basic types of decision, the executive decision and the policy decision.'[45]

Trade union bargaining strategy at the workplace has always attempted to increase the area of joint regulation and therefore to bring more policy decisions under the same system of control. Therefore although a distinction between executive and policy decisions is useful, it may quite unwittingly appear to challenge

141

the role of the trade union as a bargaining agent. Perhaps a blurring of the issues may facilitate the development of schemes for participation. Mr. Cadbury remarks that on reading

'the literature on participation, I was struck by the lack of analysis of the way in which policy decisions are made in practice. The impression given is that policy decisions are simply high level executive decisions, which might be taken at a board meeting after the circulation of a paper summarising the facts, figures and arguments . . . It is the time scale of policy decisions and the way they are arrived at, that make them difficult to fit into a participative system, yet they are an essential aspect of participation, because once taken they set the limits for executive decisions.'[46]

Nearly all the TUC and Labour Party statements on industrial democracy have, in recent times, made the assumption that participation will supplement collective bargaining; certainly that it will in no way detract from the trade union's position in bargaining. How might this situation be achieved? The time-scale which applies to policy-making decisions is very different from the fairly immediate and clearly understood time limits that exist in the bargaining process. Participation in policy decision-making may well detract from a union's bargaining position, except where new information became available which more clearly identified the management's negotiating position. It is this that gives rise to much management reluctance to develop schemes for wider participation.

Under any new scheme for increasing employee participation the position of the senior executive becomes increasingly more ambigious. In Western Germany, where wide-ranging Works Council legislation exists, the proposed extension of co-determination has focused on this topic. In a recent judgement the Federal Labour Court has attempted to clarify the position of the senior executive more precisely. They conclude

'. . . the tasks of the executive must be distinctly managerial by nature . . . the duties of the executive must stand in such a relation to the employer, so that in cases of conflicts of interest between the management and the work-force, the executive stands on the side of the management.'[47]

What are the implications of this for the British situation? At present this German judgment would probably meet with considerable support. In the last four years, with the passing of the Industrial Relations Act, a number of 'professional unions', for example the United Kingdom Association of Professional Engineers,

> 'have attempted to gain recognition from employers often by using the not very generous provisions and procedures of the Industrial Relations Act. For a body, such as UKAPE, the dilemma has been one of professionalism versus effectiveness in bargaining.'[48]

If we adopted the ideas implicit in the German Labour Court judgement then some of the objections which might exist towards extending managerial unionisation might be further reduced. In particular if there were also some recognition of paragraph 27 of the code of Industrial Relations Practice . . .

> 'A professional employee who belongs to a trade union should respect the obligations which he has voluntarily taken on by joining the union. But he should not, when acting in his professional capacity be called upon by his trade union to take action which would conflict with the standards of work or conduct laid down for his profession . . .'[49]

With an organisation which operates a participative system one cannot envisage many situations in which a professional employee as a member of a unionised managerial group would be faced with such conflict. In many instances a recognition of his professional role and its obligations would be eased by greater contact with employees from other areas within the company. The negative effects of isolation would be reduced. Where his advice and support was asked for by a large number of people within the company one could expect his influence to increase. Participation can strengthen professionalism because its contribution would

143

in most instances be more acceptable to other members of the
organisation. As Mr. Cadbury points out, 'participation is not
simply a euphemism for forming a pressure group . . . participation
in decision-making involves taking responsibility for reaching a
decision.' Perhaps it would be more accurate to say that under a
participative system the senior executive's position would, in the
main, not be radically altered but that, in addition, a new measure
of accountability would be introduced. Its principal characteristics
would be that it was 'internal', i.e. to the other participants within
the organisation. In some instances it could involve an annual
'vote of confidence' which might further legitimise the authority
given to managers making executive decisions. Presumably trade
unions for their part would have to decide whether or not
to assume some measure of shared responsibility because as
Adrian Cadbury so clearly argues, 'representation is not
participation and participative management requires decisions.'

In the UK the machinery of collective bargaining is based
upon assumptions about representation. It will require a
considerable effort by managements and trade unions to modify
existing procedures of collective bargaining so that they
complement one another. It may be that participative schemes
can adjust more easily to the existing framework of
workplace industrial relations. There may however be considerable
frictional conflict because many managers would prefer to see a
reduction in both the volume and scope of plant bargaining. They
feel that many issues now dealt with by shop stewards could
equally well be resolved through the new procedures for
participation. Industry-wide bargaining is becoming comparatively
weak, a development which is now almost taken for granted. If
another incomes policy were to emerge it could quite easily seek
to make industry bargaining more effective. Such action, if
combined with the general threat of legislation aimed at protecting
individual job rights, might provide a major impetus for change
and the implementation of a two-tier board system. Either collective
bargaining or schemes for participation will suffer if they are forced
to coexist alongside one another as a result of pre-emptive government

144

legislation. Unless innovation in this field recognises the inherent weakness of attempting to 'mass produce' participative schemes, what emerges may be an exacerbation of all the conditions that such schemes seek to resolve.

The New Environment for Bargaining

Voluntarism as the principal characteristic of British industrial relations was attacked with statutory incomes policies and industrial relations legislation. I have assessed the consequences for the enterprise and the economy. Adrian Cadbury's realistic assessment of participators can be linked to their developments in the British industrial relations system. Alan Fisher, analysing the social contract, comments,

'The search for a new interpretation of the social contract specifically related to industrial relations appears to signify an unstated acceptance of the fact that in a complex industrial society, such as ours, the primary social power is to be found at the point of production in the workplace.'[50]

It must be assumed that schemes for increasing participation must cope with this 'reality'. If they do not and the blame can be attributed in the main to management, it is likely that such schemes will be superceded by demands for workers' control. If trade unions frustrate legitimate aspirations for participation by insisting on a dominant position they will risk retaliatory legislative action. Neither of these situations could give much cause for comfort. Throughout this chapter we have been concerned with analysing the experiences of the last decade and this is relevant in examining the trade union response to the multinational corporation. In a recently published study of the relationship between multinational corporations and the Labour Government from 1964-70, Michael Hodges has suggested that:

'In most respects the Labour Government did not seek to differentiate between foreign-owned and domestic business enterprise in the formulation and execution of its economic policies . . . The instability of sterling and the

145

persistent balance of payments deficit of the 1964-8 period made
it even less likely that the Labour Government would eschew
the short-term benefits of direct investment . . . in favour of
long-term economic autonomy.' [51]

The Labour Government was not therefore in a particularly powerful
position; nevertheless it attempted to develop a policy which aimed
at establishing some form of control. In the main this involved the
creation of countervailing British firms with the aid of the Industrial
Reorganisation Corporation. By 1970, Hodges suggests, the Wilson
administration was 'on the point of spreading from consideration
of certain industries to a more general consideration of the effects of
the multinational companies on tradition methods of economic
management; the Conservative Government which succeeded it did
not develop this approach.' [52] With a Government that was relatively
powerless or indifferent it is the trade union movement that has
responded to the multinational company with demands for collective
bargaining and government political and economic controls. Its
attitudes and experience have resulted in the faltering development
of a policy whose objectives are fairly clear and whose tactics in
achieving them are immensely flexible.

Mr. Whitty clearly describes how trade unions have developed two
methods of responding to the multinational firm. In some senses both
are traditional; the first is by seeking to develop effective forms of
collective bargaining with the multinational company. The second is
to lobby governments, irrespective of their political complexion, for
various forms of governmental action. Nevertheless a number of
quite specific industrial relations questions remain. From the trade
union point of view the key problem of coping with the
multinational lies in its ability to shift its production or operations,
either provisionally or permanently, from one country to another.
This power can seriously weaken the trade union's bargaining position
and reduce the effectiveness of strike action. This situation may hold
now but there are a number of indications that the Labour Government
may seek to continue the policies interrupted by its loss of office.
The proposed National Enterprise Board is concerned primarily with
British-owned companies, but its future extension to the multinational

company cannot be ruled out. As has also been suggested earlier, the thrust of future legislation in the field of employee protection may also, because of its concern to provide safeguards for the individual, reduce the potential flexibility of the multinational to relocate its investments. The time scales for plant closures, etc., would become much longer. In part, in the area of production, trade union anxieties can be reduced but it is almost impossible to build similar safeguards in the area of management decision-making. In the case of a multinational subsidiary, the locus of management decision-making, particularly in the area of collective bargaining, is not at local level. As a result trade union negotiators feel that they have virtually no access to the key decision-makers. If participative structures are enforced, of the two-tier board variety, then some trade union fears may be reduced, although these would be precisely those which Adrian Cadbury might predict would be unsuccessful. In some instances it could be argued, for example in the case of a plant shutdown, that what is important is not the decision but the ability to implement it. The most appropriate trade union response might therefore be to extend its membership 'up' the organisation. In addition to traditional methods of organisation and recruitment of members, the unions will continue to demand government action which will neutralise some of the tactics used by the managements of multinationals to prevent their employees joining a trade union. Such legislation would create a situation in which all employees of a company now organised would jointly create demands for the effective relocation of decision-making to lower levels within the multinationals.

Earlier in this chapter reference was made to more widespread use of information in collective bargaining and the demands of many leading British trade unions for an extension of the bargaining agenda. Trade unions who seek to negotiate with multinational companies face obvious and considerable difficulties in obtaining relevant information for collective bargaining and using the data they have gathered as the basis for an extended bargaining agenda. There exists, as the trade unions see it, a dearth of financial information about multinationals as a whole and their relationship with their subsidiaries. Often the claim that a subsidiary is unprofitable is countered by references to the overall profitability of the multinational parent company. More specifically, transfer pricing can have a misleading effect on bargaining. Within the next two or three years some improvement in this situation can be expected. Membership of the EEC has begun to create similar demands for information not from the national governments, but from the supra-national agency. For example, it will demand detailed financial data, including labour costs, for components manufactured outside the EEC which are to be used in the assembly of items destined for public tenders, i.e. telecommunications equipment. Harmonisation in accountancy procedures and an emerging European Company Law will gradually result in the greater availability and usefulness of information about multinationals. The problem will then arise in the interpretation of such data.

The gradual development of an international dimension to collective bargaining with multinationals is very clearly described by Mr. Whitty. It needs to be recognised that we are not likely to see a sudden development in this field. The pattern will develop gradually and its shape will be determined by the successes and the failures of the two parties to develop collective bargaining procedures. We are a long way off from the 'clash of giants'. Nevertheless we should recognise that there is almost an inevitability about the final result. Multinationals will, within Western Europe, have to engage in meaningful collective bargaining with trade unions, because they will never cease to strive for the goal, which is the representation of the interests of their members who are also the employees of the individual companies and their national subsidiaries. The trade unions are not now standing alone against the multinationals. The have been joined by politicans and various governmental and intergovermental institutions such as the European Commission. There is a temptation to telescope the time-scale but the conclusion is clear.

How then can national governments and the multinational companies prepare themselves for this situation? Within the context of the UK the subsidiaries of foreign multinationals might be encouraged to act as a test-bed for the participative schemes suggested by Mr. Cadbury. Many of these companies have a history of innovation in industrial relations; productivity bargaining started in an American multinational. The Government should act in two ways; firstly by disclosing much more fully the financial incentives it offers to the multinational and secondly by ensuring that industrial relations legislation is observed not only to the letter but also in the spirit. Unless companies like IBM develop bargaining procedures they will face a sustained political campaign to secure their accountability by the national trade unions in the countries in which their plants are located. Trade unions will, over time, devote more resources to bargaining with the multinationals but in this they must strike a balance between servicing the majority of their members who work at national companies and the exposed minority who are employed by the multinational company. If, in the event, trade unions are not successful in developing effective collective bargaining with these companies there is a risk that political pressure groups will continue the campaign. The consequences of such a situation can provide little comfort either for the manager or the employee of these organisations.

Each of the contributors to this volume has, either implicitly or explicitly, communicated his own values and aspirations for the future development of British industrial relations. The reader may find little comfort in the catalogue of problems and the bewildering and often contradictory list of suggested solutions. Lord Zuckerman, who contributed to the first series of Stockton lectures, concluded by saying, 'But we need not, indeed we dare not, despair. We shall deal with these problems because we simply have to.'[53] This statement applies equally to industrial relations in our changing environment.

NOTES

1. K. Hawkins, 'The Decline of Voluntarism', *Industrial Relations Journal*, Vol. 2, No. 2, 1971, pp. 24-41.
2. 'The Internal Social Responsibilities of Industry', *British Journal of Industrial Relations*, Vol. 4, No. 1, 1965, p. 24.
3. Quoted in A.W. Gottschalk and L.G. Mee, 'Productivity Bargaining, the Management Function and the Behavioural Sciences', in B. Towers, T.G. Whittingham & A.W. Gottschalk (eds.), *Bargaining for Change*, Allen & Unwin, 1972.
4. Cmnd. No. 3087, para. 22, HMSO, 1966.
5. 'The Nature and Development of Productivity Bargaining', in B. Tower, T.G. Whittingham & A.W. Gottschalk (eds.), loc. cit., p. 30. Report No. 122, Fourth General Report, July 1968 to July 1969.
6. Cmnd No. 4130, para. 19, HMSO, 1963
7. In paper of A. Fisher.
8. Ibid.
9. Conservative Political Centre, April 1968.
10. In paper of L. Neal.
11. Ibid.
12. Ibid.
13. Ibid.
14. R. O'Brien, 'The Delta Rod Agreements', in S. Kessler & B. Weeks (eds.), *Conflict at Work*, BBC Publications, 1972.
15. Report No. 69, Annual Report for 1973, HMSO, 1974, para. 114.
16. B. Bracewell-Milnes, *The Pay and Price Code*, Butterworths, 1973, p. 4.
17. Op. cit.
18. *The Pay and Price Code*, para. 150.
19. Cmnd. 5429, para. 29, HMSO, 1973.
20. R.E. Walton & R.B. McKensie, 'A Behavioural Theory of Labour Negotiations', McGraw-Hill, New York, 1965, p. 5.
21. Op. cit., p. 4.
22. H. Behrend, 'The Impact of Inflation on Pay Increase Expectations and Ideas of Fair Play', *Industrial Relations Journal*, Vol. 5, p. 9, 1974.
23. In paper of L. Neal.
24. *Social Foundations of a Wages Policy*, Allen & Unwin, 1955.
25. In paper of L. Neal.
26. Ibid.
27. Ibid.
28. Ibid.
29. Commission on Industrial Relations, Final Report, para. 29, HMSO, 1974.
30. In paper of L. Neal.
31. Report No. 36, Productivity Bargaining, para. 147, Cmnd. 3311, HMSO, June 1967.
32. Report No. 31, Disclosure of Information, HMSO, 1972, para. 110.
33. *The Trade Union Claim*, p. 3, published subsequently by the Transport and General Workers' Union, London, April 1971.

34. Op. cit., p.4.
35. Op. cit., p.6.
36. ICI Limited, 'Company reply to the arguments contained in The Signatory Unions' Claim of 2nd April', 1971, p.2.
37. Op. cit., p.11.
38.. Op. cit., p.16.
39. The ICI Wage Claim, March 1973.
40. Minutes of the Negotiations, April 1973.
41. In paper of A. Cadbury.
42. 1974, p.9.
43. In paper of A. Cadbury.
44. Ibid.
45. Ibid.
46. Ibid.
47. *European Industrial Relations Review,* No.6, June 1974, pp.9-10.
48. L. Dickens, UKAPE, 'A Study of a Professional Union', *Industrial Relations Journal,* Vol.3, No.3, pp.16-17, 1972.
49. HMSO, 1972.
50. In paper of A. Fisher.
51. *Multinational Corporations and National Government,* Saxon House, 1974, p.285.
52. Op. cit., p.292.
53. 'Technological Development and its Application', p.86, in M. Beesley (ed.), *Productivity and Amenity,* Croom Helm, 1974.

INDEX

For Product Safety Concerns and Information please contact our
EU representative GPSR@taylorandfrancis.com Taylor & Francis
Verlag GmbH, Kaufingerstraße 24, 80331 München, Germany